Country Crafts for the home

Country Crafts
for
the home

Compiled by Sue Wilkinson

WHITECAP BOOKS

4975

This edition published in 1997 by Whitecap Books Ltd
351 Lynn Avenue North Vancouver, B.C.,
Canada V7J 2C4
© 1997 CLB International,
Godalming, Surrey, England

Printed and bound in Singapore

ISBN 1-55110-517-9

The Contributors

ANNETTE CLAXTON is well known as a pioneering quilt designer, trainer and exhibition judge.
JAN EATON originally trained in embroidery and printing textiles, and is the author of a number of books
on craft and embroidery.
ANITA HARRISON is an established knitwear designer, who regularly contributes a range of craft features to
leading homecraft magazines and partworks.
JANE MCDONNELL trained as a potter and has designed both studio ceramics and tableware for a wide
range of department stores in both the UK and USA.
JANE NEWDICK is the home editor on a women's interest magazine. She is particularly sought after for her
floral and herbal work.
CHERYL OWEN is a craft specialist and has contributed a wide range of original craft projects to leading
homestyle magazines and partworks. Her special enthusiasms include papercrafts and soft toy making.
GILLIE SPARGO is a freelance journalist who specialises in the painted crafts. She also works as a
photographic stylist.
PAMELA WESTLAND is the former editor of a leading women's interest magazine and now writes regularly on
craft, design and home-making.

Contents

Introduction

This book offers an exciting array of easy-to-make projects for the home, using a range of different craft skills. There's a whole host decorative of ideas – why not découpage a cup and saucer, enhace a throw with ribbons or silk paint a wallhanging? Try your hand at stencilling some cushions or even making a bed quilt. Alternatively, take a natural break to make stunning wreaths and garlands for the home, add the delightful scent of homemade pot pourri to the living room and create your own herbal bath oils.

13

Techniques

The following pages demonstrate clearly and concisely the craft techniques involved in the projects presented in the book. They include dried flower arranging, découpage papier maché and other paper crafts, stencilling fabric and silk painting as well as embroidery. Before you start any project, carefully read through the instructions for the relevant technique outlined here and practise the methods required.

Ribbon bows

Double-looped bow: *Make 2 ribbon loops on either side of your thumb and forefinger leaving a similar length of hanging ribbon on either side as tails. Cut ribbon and twist one end of a 22 gauge stem wire (page 15) around the middle. Tie ribbon around the middle to cover the wire.* **Single-loop without tails:** *As above but make only one loop and do not make tails*

Swag base

Cut a strip of wire netting 20 cm (8 in) wide. Fill with sphagnum moss, packing tightly since the 'rope' needs to be quite solid. Wrap the netting around the moss and twist the cut wire ends around the netting to secure.

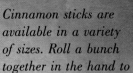

Wiring a terracotta pot

Place a small piece of dry foam into a pot so that it fits snugly. Thread an 18 gauge wire through the bottom of the pot and between the foam and the side of the pot. The pot can then be wired onto a swag base.

Wiring dried flowers, cinnamon, nuts and cones

When decorating with or arranging dried flowers, it is best to attach the flowers and other material, either singly or in bunches, to lengths of wire, since their own stems are often too thick or brittle. Wiring also helps to create a more solid arrangement. You will need 18 or 22 gauge stem wires, the 18 gauge being the strongest and used if the wire is to be the only support for the bunch.

Take a bunch of dried material and cut stems to the required length – usually 12.5-17.5 cm (5-7 in). Hold stems together tightly at the bottom between thumb and forefinger. Bend a wire about two thirds of the way along its length to form a loop. Place the loop under the bunch and hold in place with the third finger. Firmly twist the longer portion of the wire 5 or 6 times around the bunch, but not too tightly to break the stems. Single flowers, such as roses, are wired in the same way.

Cinnamon sticks are available in a variety of sizes. Roll a bunch together in the hand to make them fit together. Hold the bunch tightly, place a wire around the middle and twist the ends together several times. To wire a walnut, dip the end of a 22 gauge wire into latex-based adhesive, then push into the nut base where the two halves join. Leave to dry. Small and medium-sized cones are wired with 22 gauge wires; larger cones require 18 gauge wires. Loop a wire around the cone close to the base. Twist the ends together tightly. Trim the stems of artificial fruits leaving a short length. Wire in the same way as flower bunches or single flowers.

Binding stems

Tightly wind stem binding tape twice around the top of a wire stem or bunch to cover the wire. Hold firmly between thumb and forefinger and with the other hand pull the tape downwards so that it stretches. Turn the stem between thumb and forefinger while continuing to pull the tape downwards so that it twists around the length of wire.

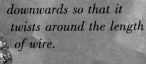

Painting details

Once the motifs are stuck down, use a fine paintbrush to paint on any fine lines that were cut off. Use ceramic paints on glass or china.

Découpage – varnishing

1 *The end result of your découpaged model depends upon how many coats of varnish are applied. Apply the varnish in as dust-free an environment as possible. Stir the varnish thoroughly but slowly so that bubbles do not occur. Dip the lower third of a varnishing brush into the varnish. Starting at the centre, brush the varnish outwards, holding the brush at a low angle and working in one direction at a time. Check that there are no drips of varnish, then set aside to dry. Placing the model in an open box will help prevent fluff sticking to the varnish.*

2 *Continue applying coats of varnish, each time in a different direction to the last. The projects in this book have been given at least ten coats of varnish. This does not give a completely smooth surface, the paper motifs can still be felt slightly raised above the surface, but they have an attractive embossed feel. After eight coats of varnish, lightly sand the piece with glasspaper, then sand again between each subsequent coat of varnish. This helps the varnish to adhere and reduces the thickness of the varnish covering the paper motif.*

Arranging motifs

Experiment with the positioning of the motifs. If the surface to be decorated is not horizontal, stick the pieces in place with plastic putty or a low-tack masking tape. Do not press the tape on firmly or it may remove the print when removed. If you are uncertain about the resulting layout, set the piece aside for a few days and then look at it afresh – you may see a solution or decide to start again.

Gluing

1 It is very important that the paper is completely stuck to the surface underneath, otherwise air bubbles will be trapped within the design, or varnish may seep under any unstuck edges. A plastic carrier bag, cut open and laid flat, is a practical surface to glue on. Use a flat paintbrush to brush the glue outwards from the centre. PVA medium can be thinned with a little water if you prefer, but do not thin it if using on glass or china.

2 Place the motif in position. Cut off any bridges at this point. If you are sticking motifs to a curved surface, cut into the design, preferably along any design lines so that the paper lays smoothly. Press smoothly outwards from the centre with your fingers, using kitchen paper towel to soak up any glue that seeps out from the edges. After a few minutes, run a finger nail around the outer edges to make sure they are stuck down.

Papier mâché – layered method

1 *Many types of paper can be used to make papier mâché but newspaper is the most versatile. Tear the paper into strips along the grain of the paper. A large, flat surface can be covered with strips 5 cm (2 in) wide but areas with corners or curves may need strips as narrow as 3 mm (¹/8 in). It may be necessary to tear the strips into squares for some models.*

2 *To apply the first layer, thin some PVA medium with a little water in an old container. Brush the solution onto the strips and lay them in the same direction across the mould, overlapping the strips. Use a knife or cocktail stick to press the strips into tight corners. Leave to dry. When not in use, cover the PVA solution with baking (aluminum) foil to prevent it from drying out.*

3 *Brush the PVA solution onto the previous layer before applying further layers. If you can use a different coloured paper for alternate layers, this will help differentiate between layers. Apply each layer at a different angle to the last to help strengthen the model. Strips can extend beyond the edges of a mould and can then be trimmed level with scissors or a craft knife when dry.*

  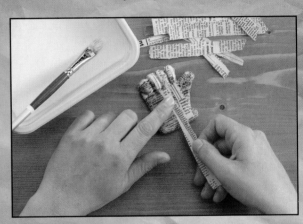

Cutting stencils

1 *Trace the templates onto plastic film, or for stencil card trace the design onto tracing paper then onto card. If details are needed, cut them from a separate sheet. Here, the cat's body and head were cut from one stencil and its eyes and markings from another.*

2 *Cut around the outlines of the design. To cut any stencil, you will need a sharp craft knife and a cutting board. Here, the stencilled design is made up of two elements – a bold cross, and delicate flowers with narrow bridges.*

Sanding, filling and undercoating

3 *These two stencils make up a teddy design. One stencil has all the body pieces separated by narrow bridges. The other has all the details that give the teddy its character. To help when tracing off the correct parts, shade in the details on the second stencil.*

1 *Using fine sandpaper, gently sand away any burrs and obvious unevenness on the model. A nail file is very useful for smaller models or corners.*

2 *If you want a smooth, level finish to the design, prepare some wood filler according to the manufacturer's instructions. Smear the filler onto the model and set aside to harden. Sand again.*

3 *A layer of undercoat will prepare the surface for painting. Household undercoat or gesso, available from art stores or suppliers, can be used for this. Apply a second and third coat if the model is to be painted with Indian inks or if it is necessary to even out the surface a little more.*

Stencilling

1 *Use a separate stencilling brush for each colour. Decant some paint into a washable dish. Dip the brush in the colour and dab off excess.*

2 *Apply the paint through the stencil with a dabbing motion, starting at the centre. Dab on other colours to give the effect of shading, or use a swirling motion with the brush.*

Fabric painting

1 *Begin by washing, drying and pressing your fabric to remove any dressing or starch. Lay the prepared fabric over the design and secure together with masking tape. Transfer the design on to the fabric using a fine-point textile marker or a sharp HB pencil.*

2 *Position the transferred fabric over a large piece of card or layer of newspaper spread on a flat surface and secure firmly in place with strips of masking tape round the edge to prevent it from moving and smudging the wet paint.*

3 *Always stir each pot of paint thoroughly before starting to work with it. Begin by filling in all the small areas of the design. Pour a little paint into a palette or saucer and apply to the fabric with an artist's small paintbrush.*

5 *Fill in the outlined shapes with colour using a slightly larger brush, then move on to outline the next group of shapes. You may find it helpful to avoid smudging wet areas by remembering to work from left to right across the design if you are right-handed. For left-handed readers, work from right to left.*

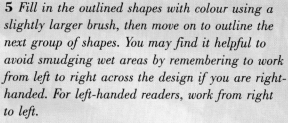

4 *Leave each colour to dry completely before applying the next. When changing colours, wash your brush and palette thoroughly in cold, clean water. Next, again using a small brush, carefully outline a group of large shapes with colour.*

6 *When all painting is complete, allow to dry overnight. To fix the paint, lay a large sheet of white tissue paper or greaseproof paper over the painted areas and press with a hot iron following the manufacturer's instructions.*

Silk painting

1 Wash, dry and press the fabric to remove any dressing. Pin the fabric to a silk painting frame or wooden stretcher using three-point silk pins in preference to ordinary drawing pins or staples which will damage the fabric by making large holes in it. The fabric should be held taut across the frame.

2 Stir the chosen colour of outliner thoroughly and transfer it to the applicator bottle. Squeeze the applicator gently over a scrap piece of paper until the outliner flows evenly through the nozzle. Apply the outliner to the fabric.

3 Allow the outliner to dry completely. Shake or stir the silk paint vigorously. Apply the first colour using a cotton bud. Soak the bud in paint, then press it on to the fabric and allow the paint to flood across the outlined shape.

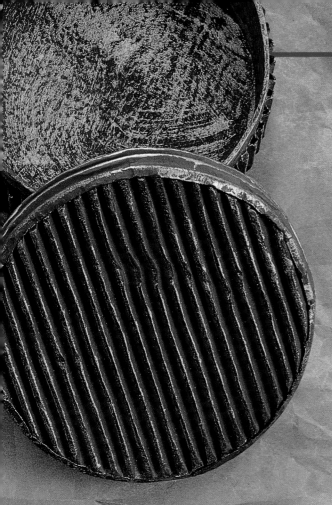

Covering a button

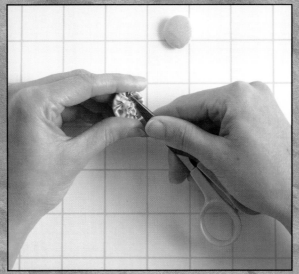

1 *Cut a circle from fabric 1 cm (²/₅ in) larger than the button. Work running stitches around the fabric edge. Place the button down on the wrong side of fabric, and the gather fabric. Push the gathered edge under the teeth on the button rim.*

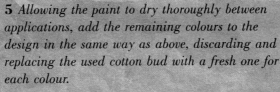

2 *Press on the button back until it clips in place.*

4 *Allow the first colour to dry for several hours, then apply the second colour using a fresh cotton bud. You will soon learn how much paint to apply, but remember that the heavier the coat of paint, the darker the finished result will be.*

5 *Allowing the paint to dry thoroughly between applications, add the remaining colours to the design in the same way as above, discarding and replacing the used cotton bud with a fresh one for each colour.*

6 *Leave to dry for 48 hours. To fix the colours, lay right side down over white tissue paper and press with a hot iron for two minutes. Rinse in cool water to remove surplus paint, allow to dry, then press lightly on the wrong side with a cool iron.*

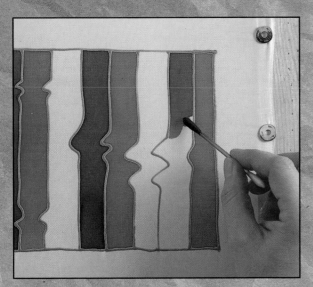

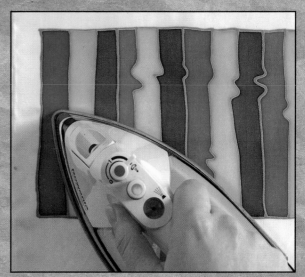

Making a round box and lid

1 *Cut card 63 x 14.5 cm (25¹/₂ x 5³/₄ in). Spray glue giftwrap to card; trim to fit on shorter edges leaving a 1.5 cm (³/₈ in) overlap on long edges. Stick double-sided tape to overlaps and one end.*

2 *Snip one overlap at 6mm (¹/₄in) intervals. Cut a card and a paper circle 19.5 cm (7 ⁵/₈ in) in diameter and attach the snipped edge to the card underside. Stick the overlapped edges together. Snip the upper overlap at 3 cm (1¹/₄ in) intervals and attach to the inside of the box. Spray glue the paper circle to the box base. For the lid cut a 20 cm (8 in) diameter card circle and a 23 cm (9¹/₄ in) diameter circle of giftwrap. Cut a card strip 64 x 3.5 cm (25³/₄ x 1¹/₂ in) for rim.*

3 *Spray glue paper lid to card lid; snip overlap at 6 mm (¹/₄ in) intervals. Wrap rim around lid and stick. Cut a strip of giftwrap 64 x 5 cm (25¹/₂ x 2 in). Glue to rim outside, sticking excess inside.*

Embroidery - running stitch

Running stitch is easy to work and looks good when the stitches are worked to an identical length. Also use as a strengthening stitch round cutwork designs. Work from right to left, picking up the fabric with an in-and-out movement.

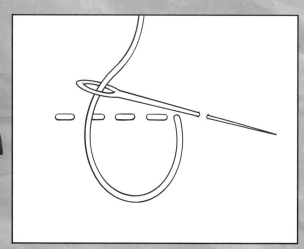

Back stitch

Back stitch is very versatile - it makes a fine, delicate line of stitching which follows intricate designs well and it is also used to add linear details and outlines to cross stitched designs. When outlining cross stitch, it is often best to use a slightly finer thread for the back stitches – where the cross stitches are worked with three strands of stranded cotton, for example, use two strands for the accompanying back stitches. This prevents the cross stitched design being pulled out of shape.

Work back stitch from right to left, making small, even stitches which are worked forwards and backwards along the row. On plain fabric, keep the stitches small and regular so the line looks like machine stitching. On evenweave fabric, make each stitch cover the same number of fabric threads for woven blocks as each cross stitch.

Blanket stitch

Blanket stitch is worked in the same way as buttonhole stitch (right), but here the stitches are spaced out evenly along the row. The stitch has a long history and the name comes from its traditional use as a finishing stitch for the edges of woven blankets. Today, it is used in appliqué and also as a decorative stitch in its own right.

Work blanket stitch from left to right, pulling the needle through the fabric over the top of the working thread to make a looped edge. Space the stitches evenly along the row or to create a more decorative effect, change the length of the upright stitches to make them alternately long and short, or add a French knot (page 26) worked in a contrasting colour to the top of each upright.

Buttonhole stitch

Buttonhole stitch, as well as being used as a decorative free embroidery stitch, makes a durable finish along a raw fabric edge. Although knotted variations such as tailor's buttonhole stitch are more hardwearing when working garment buttonholes, ordinary buttonhole stitch is perfect for cutwork, in which areas of the fabric are cut away to form an intricate design. The edges of the design are first strengthened with rows of running stitch (left) before the buttonhole stitches are worked. A flat, untwisted embroidery thread, such as stranded cotton, will give a closer finish than a rounded, twisted thread. Work from left to right, pulling the needle through the fabric over the top of the working thread. Position the stitches close together so that no fabric is visible.

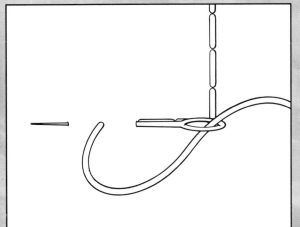

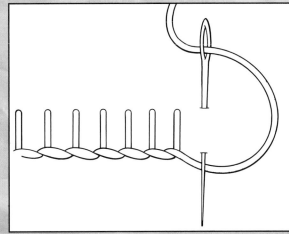

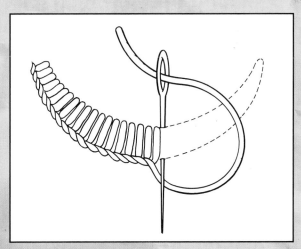

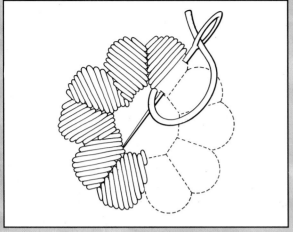

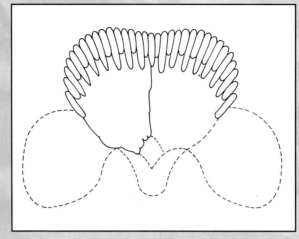

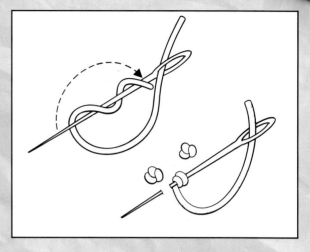

Satin stitch

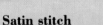

Work satin stitches in any direction as the changes of direction will create the effect of light and shade over the embroidered area. You can work the individual stitches of any length, but long stitches will tend to become loose and untidy, so you may need to split up large shapes into smaller, more manageable areas or work them in long and short stitch (right) for a similar, smoothly-stitched effect. Work satin stitch on fabric stretched in an embroidery hoop or frame to prevent puckering.

To work, carry the thread right across the shape to be filled and then return it underneath the fabric close to the point where the needle emerged. Position the stitches close together so they lie evenly and make a neat edge around the shape.

Long and short stitch

Long and short stitch is worked in a similar way to satin stitch (left), and gets its name from the long and short stitches used on the first row. A regular outline is created by the first row, then the inner rows produce an irregular line which allows colours to blend gradually into one another without a strongly defined line. Work long and short stitch in one colour to fill areas which are too large to be filled by ordinary satin stitch. Work the first row in alternately long and short satin stitches, following the contours of the shape and arranging the stitches closely together so that no fabric is visible. On the next journey, fit satin stitches of equal length into the spaces left on the first row. Continue until the shape is filled.

French knots

French knots add splashes of colour and texture to a design. Use any type of embroidery thread, but remember that the weight of your thread will determine the size of the finished knot. French knots are quite tricky to work at first and you will need to practise them in order to work the knots neatly.

To work a French knot, bring the thread through the fabric and hold it taut with the left hand. Twist the needle round the thread two or three times and then tighten the twists. Still holding the thread in the left hand, turn the needle round and insert it in the fabric at the point where it originally emerged. Pull the needle and thread through the twists to the back of the fabric.

Cross stitch

The top diagonal stitches in cross stitch designs should always slant from bottom left to top right. Work details and individual stitches by the method shown in the first two diagrams completing each cross before proceeding to the next. To cover large areas, work each row of stitches over two journeys. Work a row of diagonal stitches from right to left, as shown in the third diagram, then complete the crosses with a second row of stitches worked in the opposite direction.

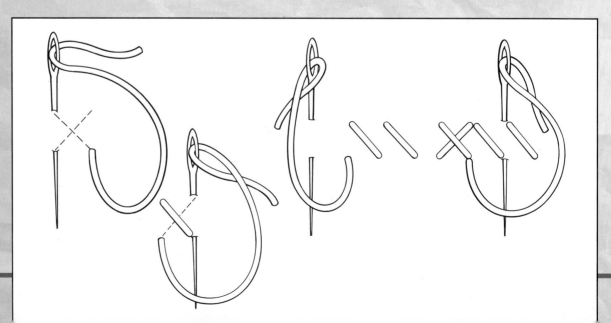

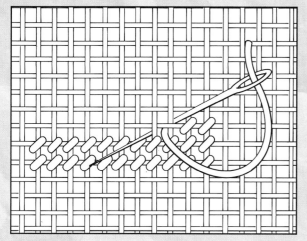

Tent stitch

Tent stitch is a small, diagonal stitch which can be used for working designs from a chart. Generally, this stitch is used for needlepoint designs and is worked with a woollen yarn. The designs in this book are all worked on plastic canvas which eliminates tent stitch's ability to distort woven threads, so this stitch can be worked in horizontal rows, rather than by the more time-consuming diagonal method. Work in rows, taking a small stitch on the front of the canvas and a longer one on the reverse.

Double leviathan stitch

This stitch is used on canvas and produces a pattern of highly raised, square blocks made up of 8 overlapping stitches. The stitch is quite easy to work once you have practised the stitch sequence a few times. When working double leviathan stitch and tent stitch (above) together on the same piece, work the leviathan stitches first, then fill in round the edges with tent stitches. Begin by working a large individual cross stitch (left) over a square of 4 canvas threads. Then work a series of crossing stitches over the top of the original stitch, following the sequence shown, finishing with an upright cross stitch. Keep the tension of the overlapping stitches even and take care not to pull the thread tightly to avoid snapping the plastic canvas threads.

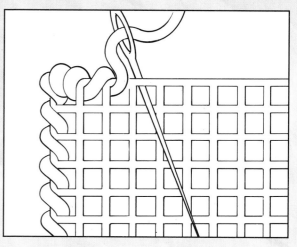

Overcast stitch

Use to neaten single edges of plastic canvas and to join two pieces together. Plastic canvas does not fray, so do not allow turnings – align edges and stitch together. Work from left to right, taking one stitch through each hole, except at corners, where 3 stitches are made into the corner hole.

Hemming stitch

Secure hems by hand in preference to machine for a neater look, although a machine-stitched hem will be more hardwearing. Turn up the hem and secure with pins or tacking stitches. Work from right to left, taking tiny stitches through both the fabric and the folded hem edge.

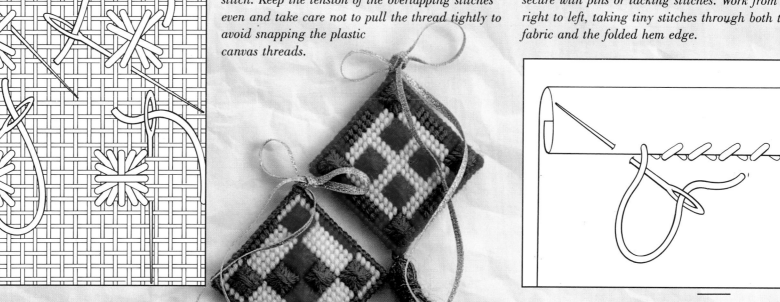

Soft Furnishings

Give your home a relaxed feel with the creative ideas found in this chapter. Make amazing
silk painted pictures for the living or dining room, then complete the look with an embroidered or
painted tablecloth. Add soft touches to the sofa with a pretty ribbon-embroidered throw and
enhance a child's bedroom with delightful teddy motif-stencilled cushions.

CLASSIC RUG

IN TERMS OF decorating, the floor is generally forgotten or the last to be considered. Yet here is a huge expanse to be played with. Floor rugs are not only functional but decorative too. They look best set against plain floorboards, where the eye is naturally drawn to them. Apart from providing visual interest, they also help to insulate and keep a room warm by blocking out cold and draughts.

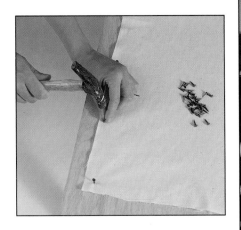

1 This rug measures 70 x 136 cm (27 x 53 in). You will need a piece of heavy artist's canvas at least 20 cm (8 in) larger all around than the finished size. Press the canvas, then pin to a large sheet of board with upholstery tacks and a hammer. Start by tacking down at the middle of each side and work out towards the corners – do not hammer the tacks in fully.

RIGHT: The simplicity of a classical design is hard to beat. The subtle colouring and geometry of the pattern fits in with most styles of decoration and blends well with furniture of all ages.

2 Paint the entire area of the canvas with white acrylic primer, diluted 50:50 with water. Paint lightly, trying not to work the paint in too hard – you do not want it coming through on the other side of the fabric if possible. Apply three or four undiluted coats, letting each one dry before applying the next.

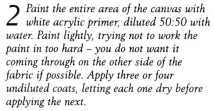

3 Pull out the tacks and trim the edges off square using a steel rule, set square and sharp craft knife. Mark a line 2.5 cm (1 in) all around the edge and another, 5 cm (2½ in) inside that. Carefully trim off each corner close to the inner marked line. Turn cloth over to the wrong side. Fold in a hem along the first marked line and then along the second. Stick hems with PVA glue. Allow to dry. Sand smooth any cracks and paint the back with one coat of primer.

4 On the right side, lightly mark a line 8 cm (3 in) in from the edge all around and another 15 cm (6 in) inside that. Run masking tape on either side of these lines, making good, square corners. Mix up a pale green glaze with 50:50 paint and white spirit. Paint between the tape. Now, dampen a rag with white spirit, roll up and run over the glaze to partially remove it.

Run tape around the outside edge. Paint and rag roll between this and the previous tape. Also rag roll the central area with grey glaze. When dry, cut stencils of the two motifs (see page 18) from the templates on page 152, and stencil with a brush (see page 20) in shades of green, dark brown and tan, using hard surface paints. Seal the surface with acrylic floor varnish.

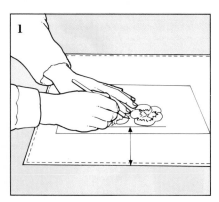

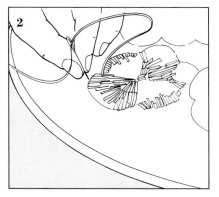

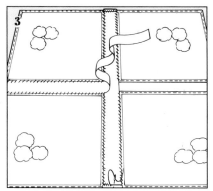

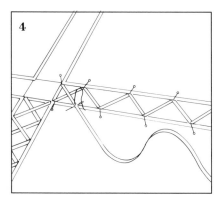

1 *Cut four 49.5 cm (19½ in) squares of embroidery linen with 27 threads per 2.5 cm (1 in). Carefully mitre the corners, then machine stitch double hems turning under 1 cm (²/₅ in) around each square. Use dressmaker's carbon paper to transfer the motif on page 153 onto each square, positioning the motif at 'A' towards one corner and the straight guidelines 12 cm (4¾ in) from the fabric edges.*

2 *To embroider the motifs use 1.5 mm (³/₅ in) wide double satin ribbon in willow (150 cm (60 in)), in pale blue (45 m (50 yd)), and in mid blue (23 m (25¼ yd)). Using an embroidery hoop, embroider the pansy motifs with long and short stitch, (see page 26). Follow the key page 153.*

3 *Cut two 105 cm (41½ in) lengths of 56 mm (2⅕ in) wide white sheer ribbon. Stitch a narrow double hem at one end of each length. Place the four squares about 5 cm (2 in) apart, right sides down, in a square, positioning the motifs at the outer corners. Lay one ribbon length face down between the squares, keeping all hems level. Slip stitch the ribbon edges to the machine stitches of the adjoining squares. Repeat with the second length laid across the first. Neaten both ribbon ends with a narrow hem.*

4 *On the right side mark points with a vanishing marking pen 5 cm (2 in) apart along the inner edges of the squares, ending 2.5 cm (1 in) from the outer edges. From 21.2 m (23¼ yd) of 7 mm (¼ in) wide white double satin ribbon cut four 150 cm (59 in) lengths. Pin the centre 5 cm (2 in) of each length between the inner fabric corners. Stitch in place. Form a lattice pattern by folding each ribbon end back and forth across the sheer ribbon and stitching in place at the marked points.*

◀ *Recreate the elegance and delicacy of a bygone era with a beautiful tablecloth made from fine linen and satin and sheer ribbons. The exquisite embroidery can be achieved by anyone using narrow ribbon sewn in long and short stitch.*

5 *Cross the double satin ribbon ends so that they meet in the middle of the sheer ribbon hem edge. Fold the ends over to the wrong side of the work, forming narrow double hems and stitching in place so that they are invisible from the right side.*

6 *Following the plan on p 153, draw lines with a vanishing marker pen on each embroidered square. Working along the outside of the lines, stitch 150 cm (59 in) of 3 mm (¹/₁₀ in) wide mid blue double satin ribbon along line 'A' and 160 cm (63 in) of the same ribbon along line 'B', stitching down the ribbon centre. Sewing along both edges, machine stitch 135 cm (54 in) of the 7 mm (¹/₄ in) wide white double satin ribbon along line 'C'. Trim ribbon ends within hem area.*

7 *Using the vanishing marking pen, mark points 5 cm (2 in) apart along the edges of the tablecloth, starting at the corners. Mark points 7 cm (2³/₄ in) apart along 6 m (6³/₄ yd) of the 7 mm (¹/₄ in) wide white double satin ribbon. Starting at one corner, take the ribbon away from the work, fold at the first mark and match the next mark on the ribbon with the next on the hem edge. Stitch the ribbon in place at the hem edge. Continue folding and stitching the ribbon where marked. Stitch the ribbon diagonally across the corners and continue folding. Press the folded ribbon. Turn under the remaining ribbon ends, overlap and stitch.*

8 *Stitching along both edges of the 7 mm (¹/₄ in) wide double satin ribbon, sew 3.8 m (4 yd 5¹/₂ in) along the inner edges of each embroidered square. Stitch a 4.05 m (4¹/₂ yd) length around the outer edges of the tablecloth, covering the sheer ribbon hems. Stitch the ribbon end over the ribbon beginning, turning under 2 cm (1 in) to a double hem and matching the edges.*

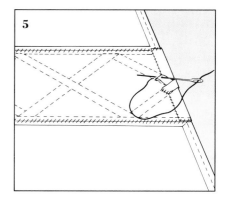

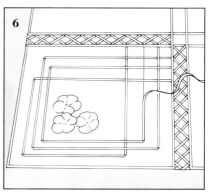

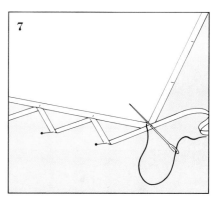

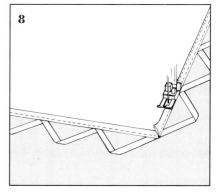

Soft Furnishings

1 *All three designs are drawn freehand and outlined directly on to the fabric. Use the close-up photographs as a guide. Following the Silk Painting technique on pages 22-23, pin the silk to the frame and draw on the design with clear outliner, working from the centre outwards to avoid smudging. Allow outliner to dry.*

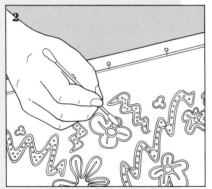

2 *Colour in the design using one colour of paint and work from the centre outwards. Allow this colour to dry, then fill in the remaining colours one by one, allowing each colour to dry, before proceeding to the next. Fix the paints. Cut out each design leaving a margin of about 1.5cm (¹/₂in) around the edge. Back each piece of painted silk with iron-on interfacing and make up the cushion cover. Insert the cushion pad and slipstich the opening closed.*

SQUARE GEOMETRIC CUSHION:
45cm (18in) square white 8
Habotai silk
Silk paints in mint green,
pistachio green, violet, purple,
yellow, maroon, pale blue,
turquoise, petrol blue,
ultramarine
40cm (16in) square cushion pad

RECTANGULAR FLORAL CUSHION:
35 x 45cm (14 x 18in) white 8
Habotai silk
Silk paints in mint green, grass
green, pistachio green, violet,
purple, yellow, rose pink,
cyclamen pink, Bordeaux pink,
pale blue, turquoise, petrol blue,
ultramarine
30 x 38cm (12 x 15in)
cushion pad

SQUARE FLORAL CUSHION:
40cm (16in) square white 8
Habotai silk
Silk paints in mint green, grass
green, purple, yellow, reddish
orange, rose pink, cyclamen pink,
Bordeaux pink
35cm (14in) square cushion pad

◀ *Make a group of
co-ordinating cushion covers by
varying the patterns, but keeping
the colours the same.*

You Will Need:
Clear outliner
Outliner bottle with fine nib
Silk painting frame
3-point silk pins
Paintbrushes or cotton buds
Fade-away embroidery marker
Lightweight iron-on interfacing
Backing fabric and sewing
threads to tone

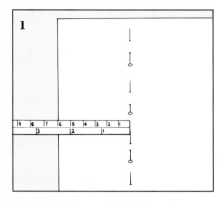

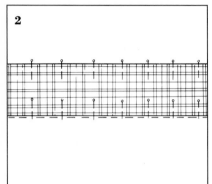

1 *From a 132 x 192 cm (52 x 76 in) length of heavyweight yellow cotton furnishing fabric cut a 112 x 112 cm (44 x 44 in) square. Press and lay flat. The ribbon is stitched onto the fabric in the position and order set out in the chart page 154. To place the first ribbon, position a line of pins on the right side of the fabric 6 cm (2²⁄₅ in) from and parallel with one edge.*

2 *With the straight-cut ribbon end to the fabric edge, place the 75 mm (3 in) wide tartan ribbon with its long edge just inside the pinned line. Pin, then machine in place with a straight stitch along the edge. Dry press on the wrong side of the work. Following the chart on page 154, sew on the ribbons one at a time, marking the position before pinning and stitching in place. Dry press after stitching each ribbon.*

◀ To make the throw you will need: 3.5 m (4 yd) of 75 mm (3 in) wide tartan polyester ribbon, 4.5 m (5 yd) of 38 mm (1½ in) wide tartan polyester ribbon, 1.5 m (1¾ yd) of 50 mm (2 in) wide rust velvet ribbon, 2.5 m (2¾ yd) of 50 mm (2 in) wide green velvet ribbon, 3.5 m (4 yd) of 20 mm (¾ in) wide rust velvet ribbon and 2 m (2¼ yd) of 20 mm (¾ in) wide green velvet ribbon.

▼ Traditional tartan and rich velvet ribbons on heavy cotton fabric make a luxurious throw to enhance any furnishing scheme. Take care to choose a colour that matches the tartan and shows off the texture of the velvet.

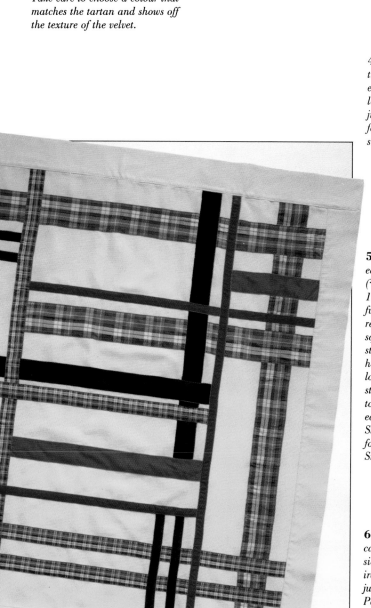

3 With right sides facing and taking a 1 cm (⅖ in) seam, pin then sew two 20 x 112 cm (8 x 44 in) strips of the heavyweight cotton furnishing fabric along opposite edges of the square. Press seams towards the strip.

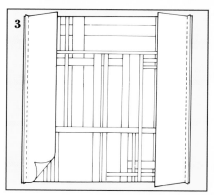

4 Press a 1 cm (⅖ in) hem to the wrong side along the long edge of the attached strips. Lay a length of strip iron-on adhesive just above the pressed seam, then fold the strip in half with wrong sides together and with the folded edge just covering the seam stitching. Steam press in place. Machine stitch the hem in place from the right side, working close to the seam.

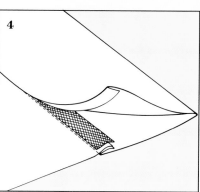

5 With 1 cm (⅖ in) overhang at each end and taking a 1 cm (⅖ in) seam, stitch two 20 x 132 cm (8 x 52 in) strips of the furnishing fabric along the remaining two edges of the square. Press seams towards the strip, then press a 1 cm (⅖ in) hem to the wrong side along the long edges of the strips. Fold the strip in half with right sides together and with the folded hem edge just covering the seam. Stitch ends at right-angles to the fold, taking a 1 cm (⅖ in) seam. Snip corners.

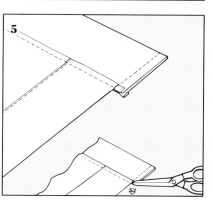

6 Pushing out the corners carefully, turn the borders right side out. Place a length of strip iron-on adhesive along the seam, just covering the stitching. Position the border hem over the strip and steam press in place. Machine stitch the hem from the right side as before.

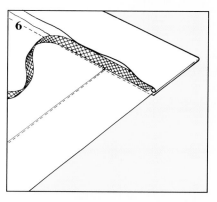

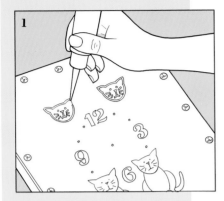

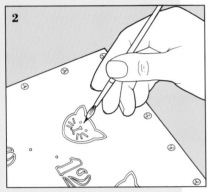

1 *Trace off the clock face template given on page 155, and transfer it to the silk. Pin the silk to the frame with 3-point silk pins. Following the Silk Painting technique on pages 22-23, outline the design with copper outliner. Work from the centre of the design outwards to avoid smudging. Allow to dry thoroughly.*

2 *Using the photograph as a guide, colour in the design with a paintbrush. Apply each colour separately, and allow to dry thoroughly between each colour. Back the painted silk with iron-on pelmet interfacing following the manufacturer's instructions. Then, following the manufacturer's instructions, mount the painted silk in the clock.*

You Will Need:
CAT CLOCK:
25cm (10in) x 30cm (12in) ivory 8 Habotai silk
Copper outliner and an Outliner bottle with fine nib
Silk paints in russet brown, blue grey, turquoise
Silk painting frame, 3-point silk pins and Paintbrushes
Wooden clock from Framecraft
(details given at back of book).
Iron-on pelmet interfacing

You Will Need:
WRAPPED VASE:
Piece of yellow 8 Habotai silk large enough to cover the vase,
plus about 10cm (4in) extra all round
Clear outliner and an Outliner bottle with fine nib
Silk paints in dark grey, orange, salmon pink
Silk painting frame, 3-point silk pins, Paintbrushes or cotton buds and Eye droppers
Vase about 18cm (7in) high with neck, Length of 1.5cm (½in) wide braid to tone
Large rubber band, PVA craft medium, Old paintbrush and an Old saucer

◀ ▶*Four happy cats decorate a wooden mantle clock, making a perfect gi▢ for any cat lover. Wrappin▢ a vase is a great way to hide any ugly or chipped ▢*

Soft Furnishings

1 *Pin the fabric in the frame using 3-point pins. Following the technique for Silk Painting on pages 22-23, draw spirals of clear outliner at random across the silk, making sure that the end of each spiral is closed with outliner. Allow to dry, then paint the spirals dark grey. Using the eye droppers, drop spots of orange and salmon pink on to the yellow background. Allow to dry, then fix the paint.*

2 *Pour some PVA into the saucer and dilute with cold water to the consistency of thin cream. Stand the vase at the centre of the silk, pull the fabric up to the top of the vase and secure with a rubber band. Cut away the surplus, leaving about 2.5cm (1in) protruding at the top of the vase. Using the old paintbrush, saturate the fabric at both sides of the rubber band with PVA. Press the surplus fabric inside the vase, and add more PVA to stick it in place. Stick the braid round the neck, and leave to dry.*

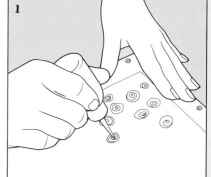

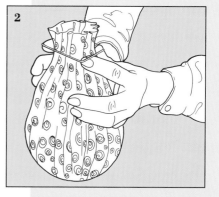

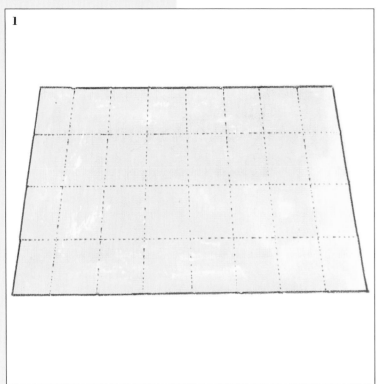

1

You Will Need:
1.8 m (2 yd) white or cream
cotton fabric 114 cm (45 in)
wide, cut into two pieces for the
top and the backing
100 x 90 cm (40 x 36 in)
wadding
1 reel cream cotton thread
1 pot each of fabric paint in
green, turquoise, yellow, blue
2 pots fabric paint in white
1 small roller and 2 sponge
covers – 1 double, 1 single
Paintbrush
A large piece of plastic (split a
plastic bag at the sides)
Masking tape
Jam jar of water
Flat plate
Hair dryer

1 *Press guidelines into one of the
pieces of fabric, folding the fabric
in half lengthways and folding in
half again, so that three evenly
spaced lines are pressed into the
fabric. Repeat widthways, folding
in half three times to make seven
cross lines. Tape an old blanket or
large piece of felt to a table, then
cover with a piece of plastic
slightly larger than the quilt
fabric. Tape the fabric over the
plastic.*

▶ *Sponge painted stripes in
bright and breezy colours add a
touch of sunshine to this bed quilt.*

2 *Cut the sponge rollers into two 2.5 cm (1 in) widths and a 5 cm (2 in) width. The double rollers are used for the green and yellow stripes; the single roller for the blue and turquoise stripes.*

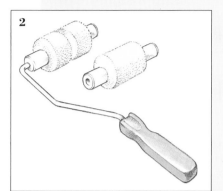

3 *Pour the pot of yellow paint into a jam jar and add one third from one pot of white paint. Mix well, then put some onto a large flat plate. Roll some paint onto the double roller, centre the roller over the centre fold and paint yellow stripes on either side of the fold. Paint with a firm but gentle touch, refilling the roller around halfway up the line. Any light patches can be touched in with the paintbrush. Repeat for the other two pressed lines. Use the 5 cm (2 in) roller to paint lines in blue paint (with a third of the white paint added) between and either side of the yellow lines. Leave the paint to dry thoroughly before adding the cross lines. A hairdryer will speed up the process. Meanwhile, wash and dry the sponge rollers. It is most important to let them dry thoroughly or the paint will bleed during the next application.*

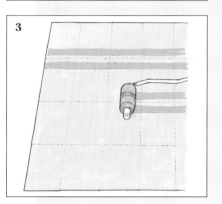

4 *Add one third of a pot of white paint to the green paint. Using the two 2.5 cm (1 in) sponges, paint lines either side of the centre and quarter lines as before. Add a third of a pot of white paint to the turquoise and, using the 5 cm (2 in) sponge, paint lines between and either side of the green lines. Follow the manufacturer's instructions for setting the paint. Prepare for quilting by pinning the layers of fabric, wadding and backing fabric together. Quilt with a straight stitch on the machine as shown in the main picture either side of the blue lines, and between the yellow and green double lines. Use a walking foot and toning cream thread, and use the side of the machine foot as a guide along the edges of the painted strips. Bind the quilt with binding tape folding the edges towards the back.*

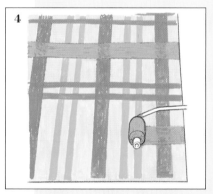

IVY-LEAF
TIE-BACK

I F STENCILLING a whole curtain
sounds a little daunting, try making
tie-backs first. They are a quick and
easy accessory to make from scraps of
fabric left over from soft furnishing
projects. Alternatively, make them in a
toning colour, as shown here, or use a
contrasting fabric for dramatic effect.

*BELOW: If the brush is still wet after
stencilling the tie-back fabric, continue the
pattern along the wall to create a dado! A
small repeating design like this breaks up a
flat, coloured wall beautifully.*

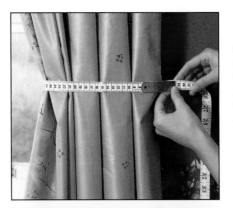

*1 LEFT: Plain ready-made curtains are
ideal subjects for stencilling. Here the
main motif is stencilled on the inside border
edge and the remaining area covered with a
tiny pattern of berries. Use the template on
page 152 to cut an ivy leaf stencil from
acetate (see page 18). Stencil with fabric
paints in soft green, green, red, yellow,
orange and white, using a stencil brush
(see page 20). Keep the stencil in place on
the fabric with spray adhesive. For the
tie-back, measure around your curtain with
a tape measure to find the length of fabric
required. Add 3 cm (1⅛ in) hem allowance.*

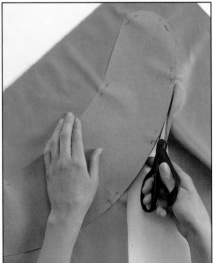

*2 Halve the tie-back measurement.
Draw onto folded paper the outline of a
curved tie-back to this measurement. Cut
out and open. Use this pattern to cut two
pieces of fabric and a lining of heavy-weight
stiffening. Use the template on page 152 to
cut a stencil from the ivy leaf and berries
motif (see page 18). Stencil onto the right
side of the front tie-back piece, using red,
yellow, orange and green fabric paints and
referring to the brush stencilling method on
page 20. Make or buy a length of piping in
a darker or contrasting colour and machine
sew around the edges of the front piece on
the right side. Cover the tie-back on the
right side with the lining and back piece.
Sew around the edge, leaving a gap for
turning. Trim the raw edges and clip the
curves, turn to the right side and sew the
opening closed. Sew a metal ring to the
wrong side of each end of each tie-back and
attach tie-back hooks to the wall.*

GINGHAM SHELF EDGING

Simple to make, shelf edging transforms plain cupboards and dressers in the kitchen, creating a sense of unity between shelves displaying a variety of items. The colour scheme used here will suit most kitchens but you may prefer to pick a colour that either tones with that of the objects you are displaying or one that reflects the colour scheme used in your kitchen.

RIGHT: Position the shelf edging just below the top edge of the shelf so that a neat line of wood is visible. This adds to the overall decorative effect. Replace the fabric lining with another paper one, or even add a third layer if the distance between the shelves is very great.

BELOW: Make a double-layered edging, backing the stencilled paper with fabric. Here the geometric design of the wallpaper is matched with similarly patterned gingham.

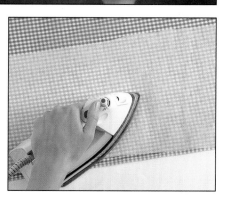

1 Cut a 6 cm (2¼ in) deep strip of green paper to the length of your shelf. Divide the length by 5 cm (2 in) to determine the number of 'v's. Mark the uppermost point of each v 1.5 cm (½ in) away from one edge, then mark bottom points. Cut out with a sharp scalpel and steel rule. Using a one hole punch, make a pattern of holes along the top edge, positioning the hole directly above the point through which to weave the ribbon and as decoration on each point. Cut a stencil (page 18) from the bow template on page 153. Stencil in burgundy using hard surface paint and a stencil brush (see page 20).

2 Choose a closely-woven green gingham fabric for the shelf edging lining; otherwise it will fray badly when cut. Press onto the reverse side of the fabric a length of light-weight iron-on interfacing as used in dressmaking. Cut as for the paper, marking the uppermost point of the 'v' 3 cm (1⅛ in) from the top edge of the fabric and the bottommost points 7.5 cm (3 in) away. Cut out carefully with pinking shears. Thread the holes along the top of the paper with three lengths of fine burgundy ribbon, one in the centre section and the others to either side. Secure with glue at the outer edges. Tie the loose ends in bows. Glue the gingham edging to the back of the paper with general purpose adhesive. Secure on the shelf with double-sided sticky tape.

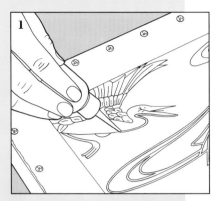

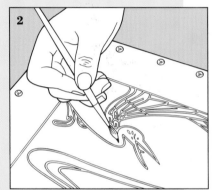

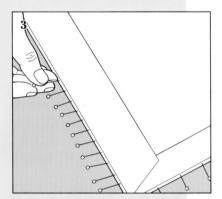

1 *Trace off the wallhanging template given on page 157, enlarge it to the correct size and transfer the design to the fabric. Following the Silk Painting technique on pages 22-23, outline the cranes and blue stripes with silver outliner. Work from the centre of the design outwards, and also outline the square containing the whole design. Allow to dry, then outline the crane symbol at the lower left hand corner of the design with gold outliner.*

2 *Using the photograph as a guide, colour in the design using one colour of paint and again working from the centre outwards. Allow this colour to dry, then fill in the remaining colours one by one, allowing each colour to dry before proceeding to the next. Finally, colour in about 5cm (2in) of fabric outside the square outline using Prussian blue. Fix the colours, then back the painted silk with interfacing following the manufacturer's instructions.*

3 *Apply fabric glue evenly to one side of the card, place the wadding over the top, press gently in place and allow to dry. Centring the design, lay the painted fabric face up over the wadding-covered card and trim away some of the surplus fabric round the edge, so the silk is about 5cm (2in) larger than the card. Keeping the design centralised, fold the top fabric edge over the card and push glass-headed pins in along this side of the picture, going through the fabric and right into the edge of the card. Repeat along the lower edge, pulling the two sides, folding into the corner neatly.*

▶ *Stylized Japanese cranes and flowing streams of water make a stunning wall decoration. Take inspiration from Japanese or Chinese paintings if you want to create a different design.*

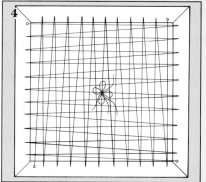

4 *Turn the picture over. Thread the needle with string or crochet cotton, make a firm knot at the end, then lace the string alternately from top to bottom until you reach the centre of the picture. If you run out of string before you reach the centre, join another length to the first one with a reef knot. Repeat the lacing in the other direction, then pull the string to tighten the fabric evenly and tie in a bow at the centre. Repeat this procedure along the remaining two sides. Stitch a small brass ring close to each of the top corners for hanging the picture.*

You Will Need:
50cm (20in) square white 8 Habotai silk
Large silk painting frame
3-point silk pins
Gold and silver outliner
Outliner bottle with fine nib
Silk paints in silver grey, blue grey, salmon pink, orange, azure blue, Prussian blue
Paintbrushes
Lightweight iron-on interfacing
36cm (14in) square thick card
36cm (14in) square lightweight polyester wadding
Fabric glue
Glass-headed pins
Fine string or crochet cotton
Large crewel needle
Two small brass rings
Sewing thread and needle

NURSERY CUSHIONS

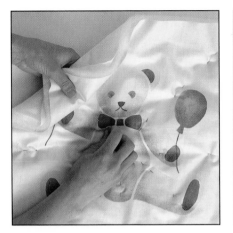 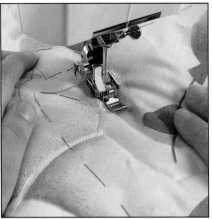 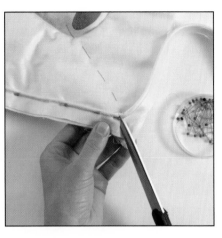

TEDDIES AND rabbits are amongst the most popular of motifs for children of all ages. Here they have been stencilled on cushions to decorate the nursery, although a little fabric ted found his way into the picture along with a tiny cupboard! Should you have a favourite teddy or toy in the house, try designing your own stencil to create a very personal and special nursery or child's bedroom. Otherwise, use the templates on pages 154-156 to cut stencils from plastic film.

1 *Wash and dry your fabric. Cut squares, circles or rectangles of fabric large enough to accommodate the chosen motif with a 1 cm (⅜ in) seam allowance added. Choose appropriate coloured fabric stencil paints and stencil the motifs onto the fabric, keeping the fabric taped down flat. Use a stencil brush (see page 20), keeping the stencil film in place with spray adhesive. Employ shading to add life and form to the teddies and rabbits, using a darker shade than the basic body colour. For a quilted cushion cover, place the stencilled fabric right side up over light-weight wadding and muslin. Pin and baste the three layers together with large stitches, starting at the centre each time and sewing to each corner and to the middle of each side.*

2 *Thread the sewing machine with cotton to match the stencil colouring. Fit the piping foot – this gives a good edge to run along the perimeter of the motif because the needle follows along the edge of the foot. Machine all around the motifs, picking out details for sewing around as well. Pull the ends through to the wrong side with a sewing needle and secure.*

3 *Use edging piping for the trim. Pin in place around the edges of the right side of the stencilled square, raw edges matching. Tack over pinning and machine in place. Remove the tacking, cut and lay the fabric back on top of the cushion front with right sides facing. Pin in place. Machine over previous stitching on three sides. Trim off excess fabric close to the piping, clip the corners and turn through to the right side. Insert a cushion pad and sew up the opening.*

4 *To make a nine-panelled cushion requires accuracy. Use a set square to ensure that corners are a true 90°. Mark the cutting line lightly with a pencil right across the fabric, then sub-divide this into 15 cm (6 in) squares. Stencil each square and join them down side seams in sets of three. Finally sew three rows together. Pipe and finish as for step 3.*

5 *For the walking teddy cushion, cut two stencils from clear plastic film (its transparency helps placement of the repeating pattern), using the template on page 155. Find fabric centre by folding in half and centre the teddy 'body' on the fold. Stencil the body first using the brush method and fabric paints in honey and brown for shading. Then use the second stencil to fill in the details in brown paint, adding a red scarf. Stencil two more teddies to either side, marking the position of the previous teddy in permanent marker pen on the edges of the body stencil to help place the stencil correctly each time. Make up the cushion as for step 3.*

LEFT: Mix images of various sizes to create interest and make objects from stencilled fabric that need occasional washing only (launder carefully in hand-wash detergent). Continue the nursery theme by stencilling other objects in the room. Here the teddies come to life marching across a pretty wall cupboard. Stencil them onto stripped and sanded wood, and protect with furniture wax buffed to a soft shine.

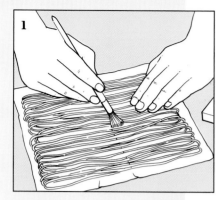

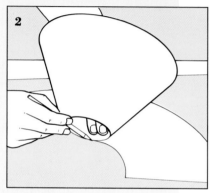

1 *Make up purple and jade fabric paint. Use cold water to dampen a 25 cm (10 in) long skein of 2.5 m (2¾ yd) of white 5 mm (⅕ in) wide double satin ribbon for the large flower motif or 10 m (11 yd) of white 3 mm (¹⁄₁₀ in) wide double satin ribbon for the allover pattern. Lay the skein on kitchen paper towels. Either paint the ribbon in a single colour, applying more thickly in some areas than in others and adding touches of contrasting colour, or paint bands of colour across the skein, allowing the colours to run into each other. Dry the ribbon with a hairdryer.*

2 *With a pencil, mark the shape of a lampshade 25 cm (10 in) in diameter on white paper, beginning with a straight line for the back seam and marking along the top and bottom edges of the shade as you roll it. Cut out the resulting paper shape.*

3 *Matching edges, fold the paper shape in half to mark the centre front. Wrap the paper shape around the shade and secure with masking tape. Sketch in pencil a four petal flower on the front of the shade, using the foldline to keep it symmetrical. Draw lines curving and looping from the flower centre in each direction around the shade, meeting at the back. For the allover pattern, alternate four petal flowers with loops in rows, leaving 4 cm (1½ in) straight lines either side of the back edges.*

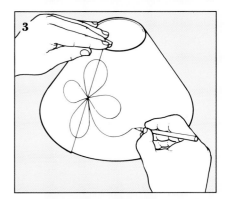

4 *Using dressmaker's carbon paper, transfer the motif pattern onto the right side of a 40 x 60 cm (15¾ x 23⅗ in) rectangle of plain mediumweight fabric. Allowing 1.5 cm (⅗ in) extra all round, draw around the fabric lampshade shape then cut out. Beginning and ending at the straight back edges, sew the ribbon onto the fabric along the motif outlines stitching along the centre of the ribbon. Fold 1 cm (⅖ in) along one straight edge to the wrong side. Press the work on the wrong side.*

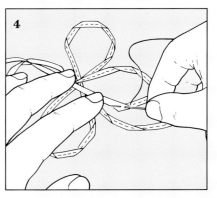

5 *Lay the fabric right side down on a flat protected work surface and spray liberally with spray adhesive. Smoothing out any bubbles, stick the fabric around the lampshade leaving 1.5 cm (⅗ in) overlap at the top and bottom of the frame and overlapping the folded straight edge at the back. Fold the fabric over the lower edge of the frame and stick to the inside. Snipping the fabric to fit, fold the top edge of the fabric to the inside of the shade and stick in place.*

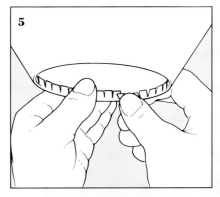

6 *Using strong clear glue, stick bias binding over the raw fabric edges inside the shade, stretching it to fit smoothly and overlapping the ends where they meet.*

▶ *Enhance a dull corner of a room with a delightful lamp decorated with a ribbon design.*

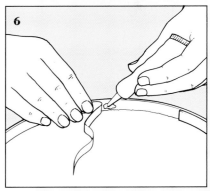

NOAH'S ARK COT QUILT

E VERYONE SEEMS to delight in making things for children. Perhaps it is just to see that look of enchantment on their faces, especially if the object depicts some of their best-loved characters or stories. This Noah's Ark quilt is bound to find a safe haven on a child's bed. Try making it into a wallhanging and a pile of cushions or stencil a border of marching animals around the room, ending at the ark.

ABOVE: To stencil the second squirrel in reverse, clean the used stencil with cellulose thinner and turn the stencil over.

ABOVE: The giraffe is positioned slightly off-centre in the fabric square. Notice the shading of the markings stencilled on it.

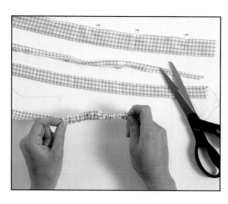

1 The tied bows at the bottom of the quilt are for decoration only. Cut six 40 x 6 cm (15½ x 2¼ in) pieces of check fabric in a contrasting colour to the quilt. Fold in half down their length and pin. Machine along one short end and down the length, taking a 1 cm (⅜ in) seam. Turn through to the right side and press well. Put to one side.

2 From plain cotton fabric, cut eight blue and seven white squares, all measuring 22 cm (8½ in) square. Cut stencils, using the templates on pages 158-159, from 20 cm (8 in) squares of card, cut to fit. Tape the squares of fabric firmly to a flat surface – kitchen worktops are ideal. Using the illustration as a guide, stencil the animal motifs in appropriate colours – yellow, brown, beige and grey. Stencil the waves, the ark, Noah and his wife in shades of blue, adding red to the ark. Use a brush (see page 20) and keep the stencils in place with spray adhesive. Note that the giraffe, and Noah and his wife templates are not centred on the square.

3 Lay the squares out in order with right sides up. Machine-sew into horizontal sets of three, taking 1 cm (⅜ in) turnings and with right sides facing. Now sew the five horizontal sets together along their top and bottom edges, taking the same seam allowance as before and with right sides facing. Press the seams open on the reverse side and set the paint according to the manufacturer's instructions.

4 For the border, cut two pieces of large-checked blue gingham 102 x 24 cm (40 x 9½ in) for the sides and two pieces 106 x 24 cm (42 x 9½ in) for the top and bottom. Machine sew the side borders in place taking 1 cm (⅜ in) seams and having right sides facing. Add the top and bottom pieces, right sides facing, joining them to the squares and the side borders and taking 1 cm (⅜ in) seams. Press all seams open.

5 *From large-checked blue gingham fabric, cut a piece for the back measuring 106 x 146 cm (42 x 57½ in), joining lengths if necessary. Cut a similar sized piece from light-weight polyester wadding for the padding. Lay the back piece out with the right side up. Over it, place the front piece with the wrong side up and cover both with the wadding.*

6 *Pin the three layers (top, back and wadding) together around the top and side edges, taking a generous seam allowance of 3 cm (1⅛ in) and leaving a gap of 76 cm (30 in) at the bottom. Trim off the excess to 1 cm (⅜ in) and cut off all corners close to the stitching line. Turn the quilt right side out. Trim wadding along the open edge, turn in 3 cm (1⅛ in) to the inside at the front and back, tucking in the three pairs of ties at regular intervals. Sew the gap closed.*

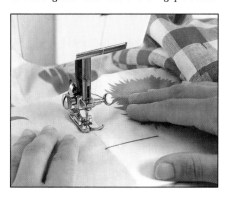

7 *Lay the quilt out flat and run large basting stitches from side to side and from top to bottom to hold the layers together firmly. Machine up and down in the seams where the stencilled squares join and similarly from side to side. Finish the machine quilting by running a line of stitching around the border, 1 cm (⅜ in) from the edge of the squares. Remove the basting and make the ties into bows. Add some quilting knots to the border. Using double thread, take a stitch through all layers on the right side, leaving the loose ends long. Take a back stitch, bringing the needle out in the same place. Remove the needle, tie the loose ends into a knot and trim. Make six on each side and four each at the top and bottom.*

LEFT: *The finished quilt should be laundered carefully in hand-wash detergent. The French metal bed on which the quilt is displayed in this picture is a photographer's prop only and is not recommended for a young child to sleep in.*

▲ *Use the close-up photograph as a colour guide, or alter the colour scheme to co-ordinate with your home.*

▶ *Make a pretty overcloth for a circular occasional table by painting a stylish floral motif in each corner of a large ready-made square scarf.*

1 *Trace off the overcloth template given on page 157. Transfer the design to each corner of the scarf using the embroidery marker, and positioning each tracing about 10cm (4in) in from the edge. Pin the scarf to the frame using map tacks inserted through the hem. Following the Silk Painting technique on pages 22-23, outline the designs with pink outliner and allow to dry thoroughly.*

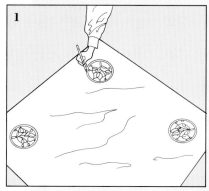

2 *Colour in each design using one colour of paint and working from the centre outwards to avoid smudging. Allow this colour to dry, then fill in the remaining colours one by one, allowing each colour to dry before proceeding to the next. Fix the paints, then place the tablecloth over a round table covered with a plain undercloth in a toning colour.*

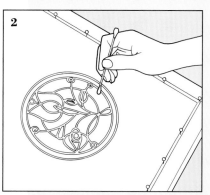

You Will Need:
90cm (36in) square ivory 8
Habotai silk scarf
Pink outliner
Outliner bottle with fine nib
Silk paints in sand, mint green,
maytime green, lavender, rose
pink, salmon pink
Large silk painting frame
Map tacks
Paintbrushes or cotton buds
Fade-away embroidery marker

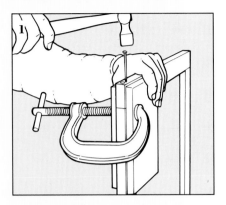

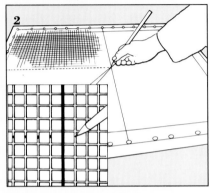

1 *Cut a 2 x 4 x 242 cm (³/₄ x 1³/₅ x 95 in) length of wood into two 57 cm (22¹/₂ in) and two 64 cm (25 in) lengths. Lay the two longer lengths horizontally 57 cm (22¹/₂ in) apart, then place the shorter two vertically each end. Place each corner between two pieces of wood and grip with a 'G clamp'. Drill two holes 2 cm (³/₄ in) apart through the side of one piece of wood into the end of the other. Hammer 7.5 cm (3 in) grip nails into these holes. The finished frame should measure 57 x 72 cm (22¹/₂ x 28³/₈ in).*

2 *Stick carpet tape over the cut edges of a piece of 55 x 71 cm (21⁵/₈ x 28 in) rug canvas with seven holes per 5 cm (2 in). Pull the canvas tightly over the frame and securely pin to the wood with drawing pins. Use a felt-tipped pen to mark the centre warp thread and the centre line of holes from selvedge to selvedge.*

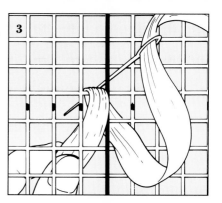

3 Refer to the chart and key on page 156 to work the wallhanging. You will need 20 m (22 yd) of jade, 40 m (44 yd) of airforce blue, 18 m (20 yd) of chocolate, 23 m (25¼ yd) of terracotta and 14 m (15½ yd) of ochre single satin ribbon, all 36 mm (1½ in) wide, and 9 m (10 yd) of 38 mm (1½ in) wide bronze lurex ribbon. Begin by working the centre two stitches on the chart at the point where the drawn lines meet. Leaving the end of each ribbon length free at the back of the canvas, work each stitch vertically over two weft threads and stitch over the loose ends at the back as you go. Complete the pattern working from the chart.

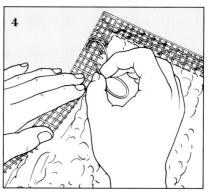

4 Remove the work from the frame. Lightly steam the embroidered canvas on the wrong side without bringing the iron into contact with the ribbon. Gently pull the canvas into shape. Trim the canvas edges to within 3 cm (1½ in) of the outer stitches and fold to the back. Slip stitch in place so that the canvas does not show around the edges of the work from the right side.

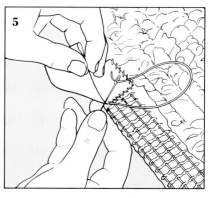

5 Cut 2.38 m (2 yd 22 in) of 36 mm (1½ in) wide chocolate single satin ribbon into 14 17 cm (6½ in) lengths. Fold each length in half widthways with wrong sides together and centre over each terracotta section along the long edges of the canvas. Stitch 4 cm (1½ in) of the loops' cut ends to the folded edge and back of the canvas.

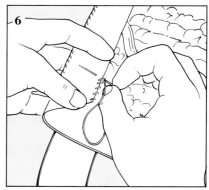

6 With wrong sides facing, slip stitch 2.25 m (2 yd 17 in) of 36 mm (1½ in) wide chocolate single satin ribbon along all four folded outer edges of the canvas. Folding the ribbon at the corners to fit, stitch the inner edges of the ribbon in place. Slip two 70 cm (27½ in) long dowels 2 cm (¾ in) in diameter through the top and bottom loops.

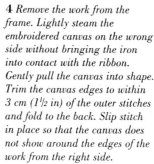

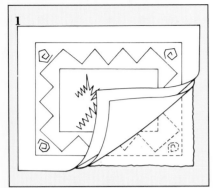

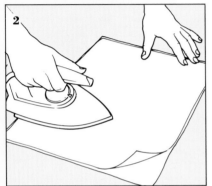

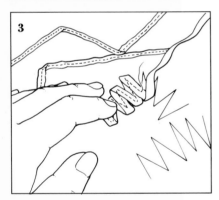

1 *Use a photocopier to enlarge the zebra motif and the elephant motif, pages 158-159 as directed. From a 40 cm (15³/4 in) and a 45 cm (17³/4 in) length of cream furnishing fabric for the zebra and elephant motifs respectively, cut rectangles 40 x 50 cm (15³/4 x 19³/4 in) for the zebra and 45 x 45 cm (17³/4 x 17³/4 in) for the elephant. Place each motif enlargement over a sheet of dressmaker's carbon paper, the carbon facing down. Centre over the respective rectangles of furnishing fabric and trace the motif onto the cushion front.*

2 *Cut a piece of mediumweight iron-on interfacing 50 x 40 cm (20 x 15³/4 in) for the zebra cushion and 45 x 45 cm (17³/4 x 17³/4 in) for the elephant cushion. Iron onto the wrong side of the cushion front.*

3 *You will need 4.5 m (5 yd) of black and 2.5 m (2³/4 yd) of terracotta single satin ribbon 7 mm (¹/4 in) wide for the zebra cushion, and 3.5 m (4 yd) of aubergine and 5 m (5¹/2 yd) of gold single satin ribbon 7 mm (¹/4 in) wide for the elephant cushion. Snip one ribbon end at an angle. Lay the ribbon over the beginning of a straight stretch in the motif and stitch over the motif sewing the stitches along the centre of the ribbon. Stitch to within a few centimetres of the end of the motif. Trim the ribbon end at an angle and stitch down, overlapping with the starting point if the pattern is continuous.*

4 *For the back, cut two pieces of cream cotton furnishing fabric 27.5 x 40 cm (10³/₄ x 15³/₄ in) and 29.5 x 40 cm (11¹/₂ x 15³/₄ in) for the zebra cushion, and 25 x 45 cm (9⁷/₈ x 18 in) and 27 x 45 cm (10⁵/₈ x 18 in) for the elephant cushion. Press a 3 cm (1¹/₄ in) hem to the wrong side along one long edge of the wider back half and 1 cm (²/₅ in) along one long edge of the other back half. Neaten both with a zigzag stitch. Using a straight stitch close to the fold, sew the narrow hem in place.*

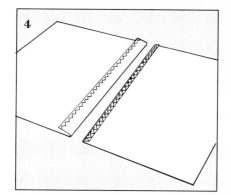

5 *For the fastening, cut a 30 cm (12 in) strip of 2 cm (³/₄ in) wide adhesive-backed Velcro. Stitch one half of the Velcro strip in the centre of the wider hem. Stick Velcro strips together, peel off adhesive backing. Overlap the two neatened back edges by 3 cm (1¹/₅ in), peel the Velcro apart and stitch the remaining strip in place.*

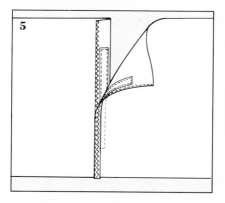

6 *Fasten the two back cushion pieces together with the Velcro. With the right side uppermost, stitch close to the edge down the fold of the hem as far as the Velcro. Stitch across the end of the Velcro for 2.5 cm (1 in). Turn and stitch back up the work. Do this at both ends of the fastening. With right sides facing, stitch back and front together taking a 1 cm (²/₅ in) seam. Snip corners and turn right side out through the opening. Press, then insert cushion pad.*

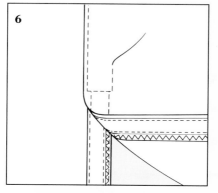

◀ *Unusual cushions reflecting the earthy colours of the African plain are quick and easy to make by machine stitching ribbon and using our basic cushion-cover pattern. Team them with natural fabrics and ethnic accessories to create a warm and colourful furnishing scheme.*

At Home with Nature

Take a step back in time to rediscover herbal delights and crafts from nature so often overlooked in this modern world. Pep-up the home with natural scents, from spicy pot pourri to sweetly scented balls. Make a restorative herbal hair tonic and relax after a hard day in a soothing, fragrant bubble bath.

At Home with Nature

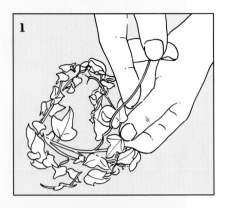

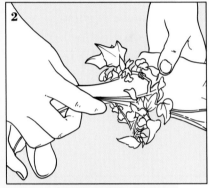

You Will Need
Slender stems of small-
leaved ivy
Florists' scissors
Silver roll wire
A short, stubby twig
Florists' adhesive clay

1 *Twist two or three ivy stems together to form a ring, and bind them together with fine silver wire.*

2 *Carefully fold the napkin and push it through the ring. Arrange the napkin neatly and twist the ivy-leaf ring to ensure that the silver wire cannot be seen.*

To make the knife-rest, twist a short, slender stem of small-leaved ivy around the twig and secure the ends at the back with small dabs of clay.

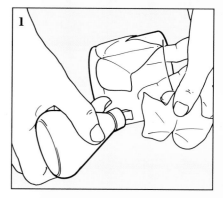

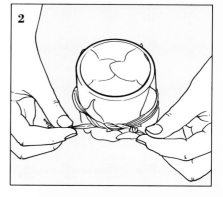

You Will Need
A straight-sided tumbler
Large ivy leaves
Clear papercraft glue
Raffia

1 *Select three or four leaves that will form a continuous decoration when glued side by side around the tumbler. Spread the glue sparingly over the back of each leaf and press it onto the tumbler.*

2 *Gather several strands of raffia together and cut the ends evenly. Tie the raffia band around the tumbler and tie a knot.*

▲ *Make the most of the ivy-leaf containers by choosing short, stubby candles. These beehive-shaped ones are made of sweet-smelling beeswax.*

◀ *Take three slender, sword-shaped iris leaves, knot them around a fanned-out linen napkin and tuck in a yellow iris flower for a simple and stylish table decoration.*

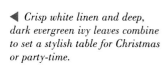

◀ *Crisp white linen and deep, dark evergreen ivy leaves combine to set a stylish table for Christmas or party-time.*

You Will Need:
250 ml (8 fl oz) water
1 tbsp sweet woodruff
1 tbsp mint
1 tbsp comfrey
1 tbsp angelica
5 tbsp pure soap
2 tbsp glycerine
2 tsp witch hazel
5 drops oil of lemon verbena
1 tbsp powdered gelatine

Makes about 350 ml (12 fl oz)

4 *When the infusion is thoroughly mixed, add the gelatine and stir until it is perfectly dissolved. When cool, pot the mixture into small jars.*

1 *This herbal bath gel is easy to make. Measure out the ingredients and boil the water in a heavy based pan.*

2 *Make an infusion of the herbs and the boiling water. Grate the soap.*

3 *Strain the infusion and discard the herbs. Add the soap, stirring well. Combine the glycerine and witch hazel and add the oil. Add this to the herb mixture.*

You Will Need:
125 ml (4 fl oz) tincture of
benzoin
50 ml (2 fl oz) avocado oil
10 drops oil of sandalwood
10 drops oil of cinnamon
10 drops oil of orange
10 drops oil of basil
10 drops oil of rosemary

1 *Combine all the ingredients
and shake thoroughly to mix
them. Only use 1 tbsp at bath
time.*

2 *To adapt the mixture you can
use different essential oils. Try
almond or apricot oil in place of
avocado.*

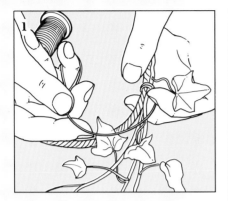

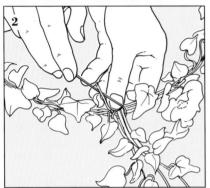

1 *Measure the coiled paper or other core material around the edge of the table and cut it a little longer, to allow for overlapping. Tie the roll wire to one end of the core, overlap the ends and bind them together to make a circle. Taking two or three ivy stems together, according to their size, bind them to the core, concealing the wire behind the leaves. Add more stems until the core is covered all the way round.*

2 *Cut off the rose stems and stick the roses at intervals around the garland. For the small table in the photograph, the roses were spaced 10 cm (4 in) apart. Choose two or three branching stems of ivy to make a central feature. Glue on a few more roses and bind the stems at right angles to the garland. Bind a spray of roses over the join.*

◀ Edge a party table with a garland of ivy and roses to give it a pretty and festive effect. The ivy trails are bound to a core of coiled paper ribbon colour co-ordinated to the roses.

To give the garland the freshest possible look, you may like to bind the ivy trails the night before the event or early in the morning and stick on the roses before the start. Lightly crush the rose stems and keep them in water until it is time to attach them to the decoration.

You Will Need
Long trails of small-leaved ivy
Roses
Coiled paper ribbon, or
string or cord
Silver roll wire
Hot glue or
clear quick-setting glue
Florists' scissors

▲ It's roses all the way for this casual hat trim. Bind the flowers and leaves to make two small posies and fix them to the hat with stub wire staples pushed through the straw.

65

At Home with Nature

You Will Need:
70 ml (3 fl oz) vodka
15 ml (1 tbsp) rosewater
1 cup scented dried rose petals
2 vanilla pods
10 drops oil of roses
10 drops oil of vanilla
10 drops petitgrain oil
5 drop oil of ylang-ylang

1 *Measure out the vodka and the scented dried rose petals, or pull the petals off the roses if they are whole flower heads.*

2 *Lightly crush the vanilla pods and steep them with the rose petals in the vodka. Cover and leave for a week.*

3 *Strain the vodka and add the rosewater. Stir very well.*

4 *Add the drops of essential oils, stirring constantly. Bottle and leave to mature for about four weeks. Strain again through filter paper and bottle before using.*

◀ *Make an impression with scent by putting on a dash of homemade perfume every time you go out. If you wish you can make the scent unique by using other flowers or essential oils.*

You Will Need:
2 fresh limes
250 ml (8 fl oz) vodka
15 drops oil of lime
10 drops petitgrain oil
5 drops oil of lavender
5 drops oil of bergamot
5 drops oil of bayleaf
1 tsp tincture of benzoin
250 ml (8 fl oz) rosewater

1 *Gather together all the
ingredients and put to one side,
except for the vodka and the limes.
Measure out the vodka into a
container.*

2 *Peel the limes and put the peel into the vodka. Cover and leave to steep for a week.*

3 *Put the drops of essential oil and benzoin into the rosewater, and stir very well. Strain the vodka and discard the lime peel. Mix the rosewater with the vodka. Stir very well and bottle. Leave for four weeks. Strain again through a paper filter, then bottle finally before use.*

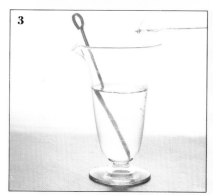

◀ *Just perfect for the man in your life, this lime skin freshener really adds a zing.*

You Will Need:
1 cup dried eucalyptus leaves
1 cup dried bay leaves
1 cup lemon verbena leaves
½ cup uva-ursi (bearberry)
leaves
½ cup dried thyme/
rosemary/sage etc.
A few whole sprigs of dried
thyme
½ cup powdered orris root
several drops of lime (linden)
flower, vervain or rosemary
essential oil

1 *Put all the leaves into a large mixing bowl.*

2 *Add the orris root and mix really well with your hands or a wooden spoon.*

3 *Add several drops of oil stirring as you do so. Put the mixture into large paper bags and loosely close them with a dog-clip or clothes-peg. Leave in a cool dark place to cure, preferably for several weeks, before using them for display.*

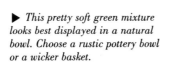

▶ *This pretty soft green mixture looks best displayed in a natural bowl. Choose a rustic pottery bowl or a wicker basket.*

▲ *Using whole rosebuds makes a more interesting, stylish pot pourri mixture than rose petals.*

You Will Need:
5 cups red or pink whole rosebuds
¹/₂ cup powdered orris root
¹/₄ cup ground cloves
¹/₄ cup ground allspice
4 drops oil of rose geranium
4 drops oil of ylang-ylang

1 *Put the rosebuds into a large bowl and add the orris root and ground spices. Mix these very well together. Add the oils drop by drop, stirring the mixture all the time.*

2 *Scoop the mixture into paper bags and fold over the tops. Leave the bags in a cool dark place for at least four weeks to cure, before displaying the pot pourri.*

71

▲ Colour-match your pot pourri to your furnishing scheme and it becomes an eye-catching accessory. This blue and cream blend includes dried cornflowers, hydrangea florets, lavender, larkspur, sea lavender, marjoram flowers, strawflowers and tansy. The added fragrances are ground ginger and cinnamon, with rosemary oil and the fixative, ground orris root powder.

Drying Plant Materials
Gather petals and flowers for drying on a dry day, and discard any blemished or damaged ones. Spread them in a single layer on a tray or in a shallow basket and dry them outside in partial shade - the traditional way - or in an airing cupboard or other warm,

dry place. Stir the materials frequently until they feel and sound as crisp as cornflakes.

You can also add any already dried flowers and leaves to your pot pourri blend. It is a satisfying way to use off-cuts and snippings from larger arrangements in a further decorative way.

▶ Making pot pourri offers you the chance to combine petals and flowers from the garden, moss and cones from the countryside and exotic and lingering aromas from the spice market. The blends shown on these pages are chosen as much for their texture and colour appeal as for their distinctive fragrances.

Green Moss Pot Pourri

1 cup deep red dried peony or
rose petals
1 cup dried green moss
1/2 cup dried eucalyptus
A few *Nigella orientalis*
seedheads
1 tbsp coriander seeds
lightly crushed
1 tsp allspice seeds
lightly crushed
1 tsp ground cinnamon
1 tbsp ground orris root powder
2 drops geranium oil
or other essential oil

*Put all the plant materials and
spices into a large container, stir
well, and add the ground orris
root powder, the fixative that will
'hold' the other fragrances. Cover
the jar and set it aside, away
from direct sunlight, for 1 week,
stirring the contents every day.
Add the oil and set aside for a
further 5 weeks, stirring each day
if possible.*

Whole Spice Blend

1 cup small pine or larch cones
1 cup dried bay leaves
lightly crumbled
1 cup dried pine leaves
1/2 cup dried rosehips
1/2 cup dried eucalyptus leaves
1 tbsp coriander seeds
2 tbsp star anise seedpods
1 tbsp juniper berries
1 tsp cloves
2 cinnamon sticks, crumbled
4-5 nutmegs
A few blades of mace
Dried peel of 1 orange
3 drops pine oil or orange oil

*Mix together all the plant
materials and spices so that they
are well blended. Add the
essential oil, and mix well. Set
the mixture aside in a lidded
container for 6 weeks, stirring it
every day if possible.*

At Home with Nature

You Will Need:
2 tsp white beeswax granules
4 tbsp apricot kernel oil
2 tbsp coconut oil
2 tbsp glycerine
2 tbsp orangeflower water
3 drops oil of orange

1 *Gather together all the ingredients and measure out the beeswax granules*

2 *Melt the beeswax and apricot kernel and coconut oils in the top half of a double boiler, over hot water, stirring until they are completely dissolved.*

▶ *Orangeflower water is good for dry skin and stimulates cell replacement.*

3 *Add the glycerine to the beeswax and oils and stir thoroughly. Warm the orange-flower water separately.*

4 *Remove the double boiler from the heat and add the orange-flower water drop by drop, beating all the time until it is a smooth cream. Add the oil of orange and stir well. Add colouring if you wish. Pot into small jars.*

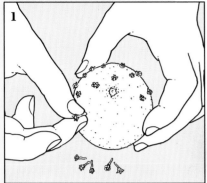

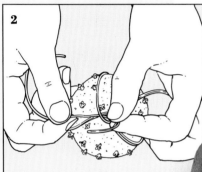

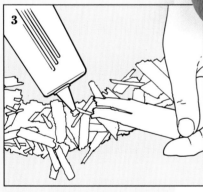

1 *Stud the oranges, limes and lemon with the cloves. If the fruit rind is specially tough it may be necessary to pierce it first with a darning needle or fine skewer.*

2 *Tie the citrus pomanders with the leather thonging, finishing with a small bow.*

3 *Cover the lower half of the stem ring with cinnamon bark or shavings, gluing the strips randomly at all angles.*

You Will Need
2 Oranges
2 Limes
1 Lemon
Cloves
A darning needle or fine
skewer (optional)
Narrow leather thonging
Long cinnamon sticks
Raffia
Cinnamon bark or 'shavings',
from Asian grocers
Exotic seedheads such as brazil
nut cases, from florists
Sprays of bay leaves
A twisted twig ring
25 cm (10 in) in diameter
Medium-gauge stub wires
Wirecutters
Florists' scissors
Hot glue or
clear quick-setting glue

▶ *Turn back the clock to the Middle Ages when homes were scented with 'clove oranges' and bunches of fragrant herbs. This tangy citrus fruit and mixed spice ring has more than just a refreshing aroma - it is highly decorative too.*

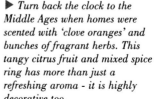

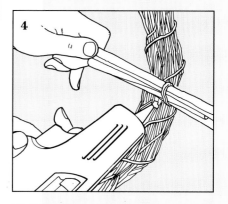

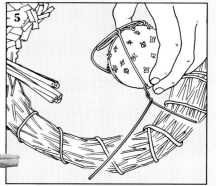

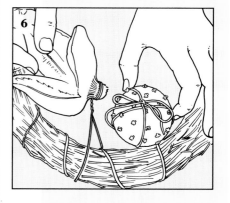

4 *Tie the cinnamon sticks into equal bundles with the raffia and glue them across the centre of the ring or fix them to the ring with a bent stub wire staple.*

5 *Push stub wires through the back of each fruit, twist the two ends of the wire and attach it to the ring.*

6 *Wire or glue the seedheads in place. Wire sprays of bay leaves on either side of the ring.*

At Home with Nature

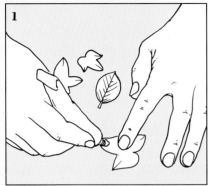

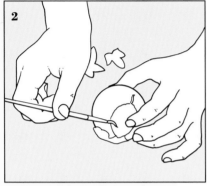

You Will Need
Selection of pressed leaves
in a variety of shapes,
sizes and colours
A styrofoam ball 7.5-10.5 cm
(3-4½ in) in diameter
Clear papercraft glue
A small paintbrush

1 *Spread glue evenly over the reverse side of each leaf. Press each one onto the ball, overlapping the leaves so that the foam is completely covered.*

2 *Use a small paintbrush to brush off any powdered fall-out from the styrofoam, and to press the leaves in place.*

▲ Small parcels wrapped in plain or textured papers have a look of individuality when they are tied around with leather thonging, raffia or string, and decorated with one, two or three pressed leaves.

◄ A patchwork of fallen leaves glued to a styrofoam ball makes an unusual decoration that can be displayed in a variety of ways.

79

Home Comforts

It is the little touches that turn a house into a home, from hand-painted orchid bowls in which to keep jewellery or other keepsakes to embroidered placemats for the table. The time and effort involved in making any of these projects is negligible compared to the effect they create in the home.

Home Comforts

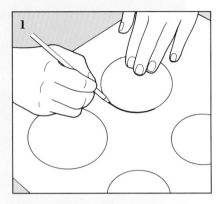

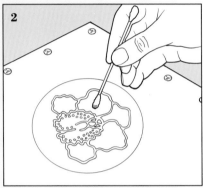

You Will Need:
Small pieces white 8
Habotai silk
Clear outliner
Outliner bottle with fine nib
Silk painting frame
3-point silk pins
Paintbrushes or cotton buds
Cut crystal bowls with silver-plated lids from Framecraft (details given at back of book).
Iron-on pelmet interfacing

CYMBIDIUM ORCHID:
Silk paints in pastel yellow, mandarin yellow, ochre, mint green

PEACH ODONTOGLOSSUM ORCHID:
Silk paints in pale salmon pink, salmon pink, Bordeaux pink, plum

PINK ODONTOGLOSSUM ORCHID:
Silk paints in lemon yellow, sand, rose pink, Bordeaux pink, carmine red

1 *Paint several bowl lids at the same time. Remove the acetate circles from the bowl lids, lay them on the silk about 5cm (2in) apart and draw round them with a pencil. Trace off the orchid templates given on pages 160-161, and transfer the designs to the centre of each circle. Stretch the fabric in a frame with 3-point silk pins. Outline the motifs and the outside edge of each circle with clear outliner following the technique given on page 22. Allow the outliner to dry.*

2 *Following the Silk Painting technique given on pages 22-23, fill in the orchid motifs and the green background with silk paints, using the photograph as a colour guide. Allow the paint to dry, remove the silk from the frame and fix the colours. Back with interfacing, then cut out each design along the circular outline. Following the manufacturer's instructions, mount the silk in the bowl lids.*

◄ *Luxurious hand-cut crystal bowls are decorated with the aristocrat of the flower world, the orchid.*

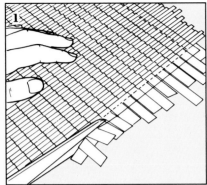

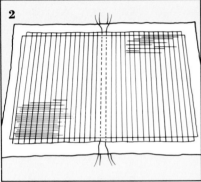

1 *Refer to the key on page 160 for ribbon specifications. Draw a 31 x 48 cm (12²/5 x 19 in) rectangle lengthways on paper and pin onto a cutting board. Pin 57 53 cm (21 in) lengths of green ribbon across the rectangle with wrong side up. Repeating the weaving plan on page 160, weave 38 cm (15 in) lengths of the sable banana and sage green ribbon across these warp ribbons wrong sides up. Pin at each end. Press lightweight iron-on interfacing over the weaving. Stitch around the edges of the weaving on the right side. Trim the edges 1 cm (²/5 in) from the stitches.*

2 *From a 38 x 75 cm (15 x 29¹/2 in) piece of green moiré fabric cut a rectangle 38 x 55 cm (15 x 21³/4 in). With wrong sides together, centre the weaving over it. Stitch along the edges of the central strip of banana ribbon to the edges of the weaving for the writing case spine.*

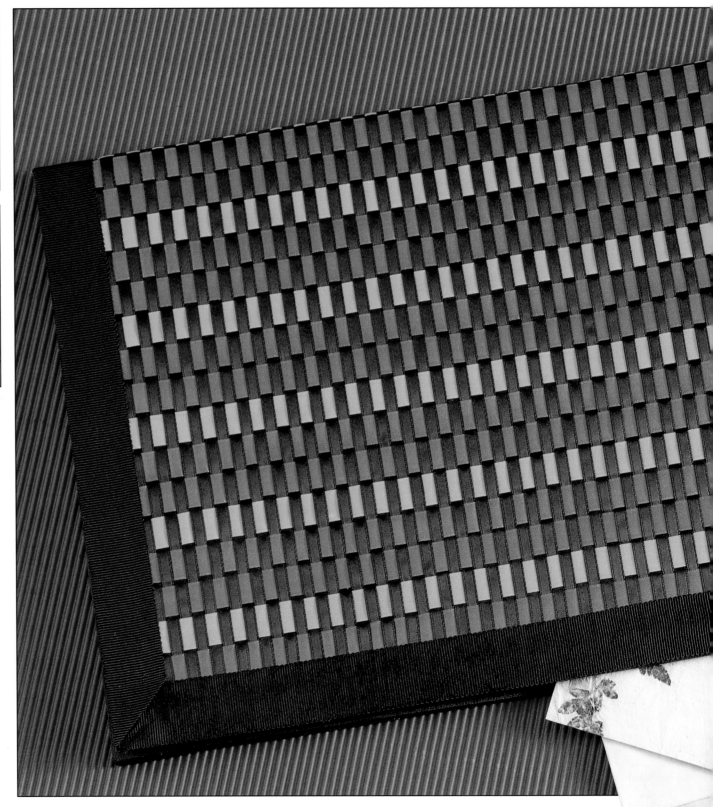

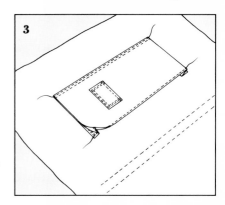

3 *Carefully mitring the corners, turn under 1 cm (²/5 in) for a double hem around a 5.5 x 7.5 cm (2¼ x 3 in) piece of moiré fabric for the stamp pocket and around a 14 x 33 cm (5½ x 13 in) piece for the envelope pocket. Sew the stamp pocket to the envelope pocket along the lower three edges. Press under 3 cm (1⅕ in) each short end of the envelope pocket. Press 1.5 cm (³/5in) of the fold back on itself.*
Centring the envelope pocket on the left-hand side of the case and working through the fabric layer only, sew the short edges in place. Stitch along the outer long edge of the pocket.

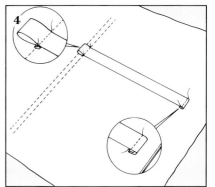

4 *From 2.07 m (2 yd 10½ in) of 25 mm (1 in) wide green petersham ribbon cut 26.5 cm (10½ in). Turn under a narrow hem each end. Stitch to the fabric 9.5 cm (3¾ in) from the upper and 2 cm (¾ in) from the outer edge. Lay the ribbon across the fabric to the spine stitching. Loop excess fabric and stitch along the right-hand spine stitching.*

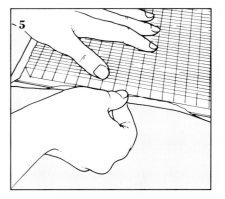

5 *Spray both sides of two 24.5 x 35 cm (9⅗ x 13¾ in) pieces of stiff card with spray adhesive. Pushing one long edge of each card up against the spine between the weaving and the fabric, stick the woven sides to the card. Stick the fabric to the other side of the card. Mitring the corners, turn and stick the fabric over the card edges.*

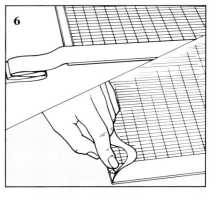

6 *Matching the edges of 180 cm (2 yd) of the 25 mm (1 in) wide petersham with the outer edges of the card, stick the petersham over the fabric and the weaving edges, neatly folding the corners at 45 degree angles to look like mitred corners.*

Home Comforts

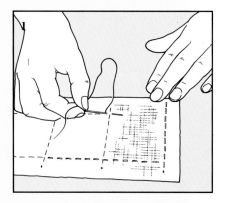

1 *Using tacking stitches, mark out 6 identical divisions measuring 25 fabric blocks square on each green fabric strip. Mark the centre of each square with a couple of tacking stitches.*

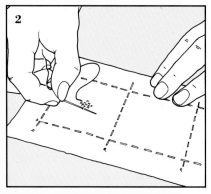

2 *Using the photograph as a guide, work a snowflake motif from the chart (page 161) in cross stitch (page 26) at the centre of each square. Then work the corresponding numbers (page 161) in back stitch (page 25) placing the numbers 2 squares inside the tacked lines. Use 3 strands of thread in the tapestry needle throughout.*

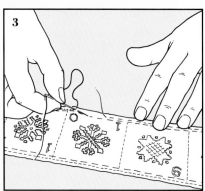

3 *Trim away surplus fabric allowing a margin of 8 blocks outside the tacked lines. Turn under 6 blocks all round, leaving a 2 block margin showing on the right side, and tack in place. Using the gold thread, work back stitch along the lines indicated by the original tacking, removing the tacking stitches as you go. Press lightly on the wrong side.*

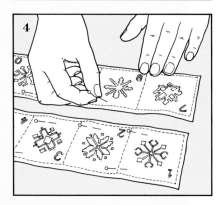

4 *Arrange the strips in the correct sequence on the white fabric, leaving a gap of 8 blocks between the strips. Pin the strips in position. Using the transparent thread, machine stitch along the sides and lower edge of each strip, forming pockets by taking the stitching up to the top edge and back down again when you reach the vertical gold lines dividing the snowflakes.*

You Will Need
4 strips 42 x 13 cm (16½ x 5 in) of green 11 count Aida
50 cm (20 in) square of white 11 count Aida
3 skeins DMC stranded cotton in white
2 spools Balger – #8 Fine Braid in bright gold
36 cm (14 in) square of card
36 cm (14 in) square of thin wadding

Tapestry needle size 24
Sewing needle
Transparent machine thread
Tacking thread in a light colour
Fine string or crochet cotton
Fabric glue
Glass-headed pins
Large needle with long eye
2 small brass rings
24 small gifts
Gold wrapping paper

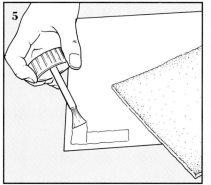

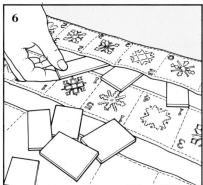

5 Spread fabric glue over one side of the card. Lay the wadding over the card, matching the sides, and gently press in place. Allow the glue to dry thoroughly. Following the instructions on pages 92-93, lace the white fabric over the padded card with string or crochet cotton. Leave a margin of 3 fabric blocks showing round the sides and along the lower edge and 2 blocks along the top edge.

6 Stitch a brass ring securely to the top corners on the back of the calendar. Wrap the gifts neatly with gold paper and tuck a gift into each pocket. Tap two picture pins into the wall to correspond with the rings and hang up the calendar, or stand the calendar on a shelf or piece of furniture.

◀ Wrap 24 presents and open one on each day of December until the big day finally arrives! Tiny notebooks, chocolate bars, puzzles and packs of small coloured pencils make good gifts.

GARDEN SCREEN

UNLESS YOU are guaranteed beautiful weather all year round, when it is always possible to step out into the garden, it is a pleasant idea to bring a little of the garden indoors. A screen is the perfect medium for this as, stencilled with a garden motif, it can grace any room from a conservatory to a bedroom. Use it to disguise unsightly views or purely as a decorative room divider.

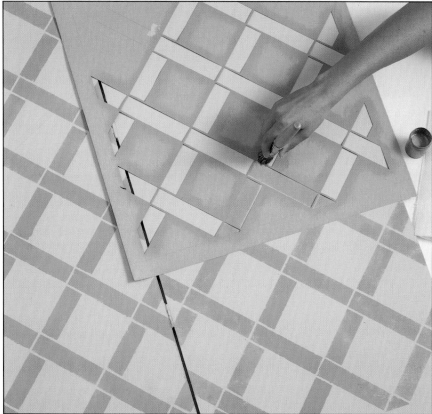

1 *Measure the dimensions of your screen and, on a large piece of stencil card, mark the width of the screen panels. Use the template on page 160 to trace and cut out an area of trellis stencil, which fits the width, (see page 18). Follow the illustration as a guide. Starting approximately 18 cm (7 in) from the bottom of your screen, stencil the*

trellis in soft brown hard surface paint unevenly applied. Use a stencil brush following the method on page 20. Register the stencil by laying the centre bottom slats over the trellis peak you have just painted. Match up the slats at the sides of each panel, but do not worry if you cannot do this exactly.

2 *Join several sheets of stencil card together to cover the area of one panel. Trace the container template on page 160 onto the bottom of the card. Draw in a topiary tree approximately 75 cm (29¹/₂ in) in height, following the illustration as a guide and leaving stencilled bridges (see page 18) between the trunk and foliage. Add climbing ivy down one side. If you do not feel your drawing is up to it, pick various-sized ivy leaves from your own or a friend's garden and use them to trace around, making a random pattern. Leave a bridge down the middle of some leaves to indicate veining. Cut out your stencil and position it on one outside panel with spray adhesive. To recreate the texture of a topiary bush, use a sponge (see page 20) to apply several shades of green hard-surface paint on top of one another, keeping the colour denser down one side of the tree and at its base. Stencil the trunk in mid brown.*

3 Paint the container in terracotta, using the brush method (see page 20) and lightly speckling small areas in a darker brown on a sponge. Stencil a second tree omitting the smallest ball at the top. Use the templates on page 161 to cut a pot stencil and position it between the two trees. Stencil the pots in the same colours used for the topiary tree container, again speckling the pots with a darker brown paint applied with a sponge. Use the brush method to paint the herb leaves in green, adding touches of yellow and brown. Use a grey-green paint for the leaves of the sage and stencil the flower heads in purple with touches of red.

4 Cut out stencils for the hanging basket and the butterfly using the templates on page 156. Stencil the basket mesh in brown, unevenly applied with a brush. Use several shades of green with touches of brown and yellow to stencil the trailing geraniums leaves, and light green, grey and yellow for the tradescantia leaves. Draw veins on some of the leaves with a brown permanent marker pen. Stencil the geranium flowers in shades of red, using white highlights. Mix red and white for one flower to create pink geranium heads. Stencil the allium in yellow. Use yellow, red, blue and dark brown paints to stencil the butterfly.

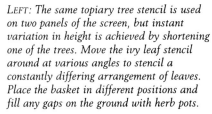

LEFT: The same topiary tree stencil is used on two panels of the screen, but instant variation in height is achieved by shortening one of the trees. Move the ivy leaf stencil around at various angles to stencil a constantly differing arrangement of leaves. Place the basket in different positions and fill any gaps on the ground with herb pots.

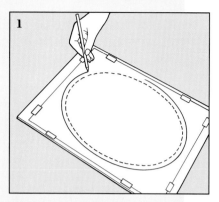

1 *Following the manufacturer's instructions, take the tray to pieces. Place the top board (with the cut-out oval) on a flat surface and centre the piece of silk on top. Secure with masking tape. Using the marker, carefully draw round the aperture 1.5cm (^{1}/$_2$in) from the edge to make a large oval outline on the fabric.*

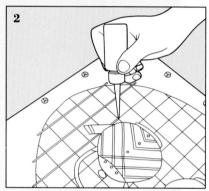

2 *Trace off the teapot template given on page 163, and transfer to the fabric using the embroidery marker, making sure that the chequerboard pattern meets the oval outline. Pin the fabric in the frame with 3-point silk pins. Outline the teapots, chequerboard background and the outside edge of the oval with clear outliner following the technique given on page 22. Allow the outliner to dry.*

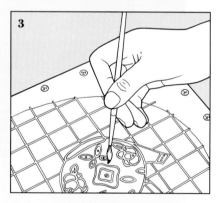

3 *Following the Silk Painting technique on pages 22-23, fill in the teapot design and background with paints, using the photograph as a guide. Allow the paint to dry, remove the silk from the frame then fix following step 6 on page 23, or according to the manufacturer's instructions. Cut out the design leaving a margin of 1.5cm (^{1}/$_2$in) around the edge.*

You Will Need:
40 x 55cm (16 x 22in) white 8
Habotai silk
Clear outliner
Outliner bottle with fine nib
Silk paints in carmine red, old
gold, ice blue, mid blue,
ultramarine blue
Silk painting frame, 3-point silk
pins and Paintbrushes
Rectangular wooden tray from
Framecraft (details at back.)
Lightweight iron-on interfacing
Fade-away embroidery marker

▶ *Just the thing for tea for two, this charming design is cleverly mounted in a wooden tray. To keep the silk clean, the tray comes complete with a sheet of glass.*

4 Back the painted silk with iron-on interfacing following the manufacturer's instructions. Place the top board over the white card supplied with the tray and lightly draw round the oval with a pencil. Remove the top board. Lay the painted silk right side up over the white card, centring the design over the drawn oval. Secure in place with strips of sticky tape. Re-assemble the tray.

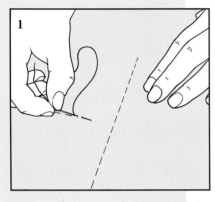

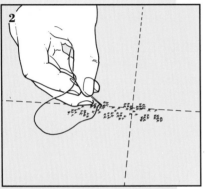

1 *Tack a horizontal and vertical line across the fabric to find the centre. Also find the centre of the chart on page 162, and mark this with a soft pencil (the mark can be erased later). Mount the fabric in an embroidery hoop.*

2 *Work the design in cross stitch (page 26) and back stitch (page 25) from the chart. Use 3 strands of cotton and one strand of gold braid for the cross stitch, and 2 strands of cotton for the back stitch. Work French knots (page 26) in 3 strands of red thread to make the holly berries on top of the puddings, and French knots in 2 strands of grey thread for Santa's eyes.*

You will need

40 cm (16 in) square of antique white 11 count pearl Aida
DMC stranded cotton in the following colours: 1 skein each of yellow 972; bright red 606; flesh pink 353; yellow green 702, mid green 367; brown 610, chestnut brown 975, golden brown 976; dark grey 3799
2 skeins of bright red 666; mid blue green 911
1 spool Balger – #8 Fine Braid in gold
Tapestry needle size 24
Sewing needle
Tacking thread in a dark colour
Embroidery hoop
32 cm (12¹/₂ in) square of thick card
Fine string or crochet cotton
Glass-headed pins
Large needle with long eye

▼▲ *Make the tiny pictures by working individual cross stitch motifs and mounting them in small gold frames.*

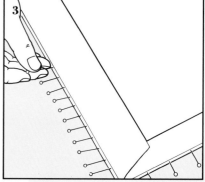

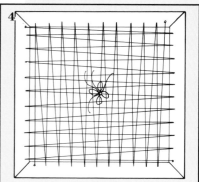

3 When the embroidery is completed, press lightly on the wrong side. Lay it centrally over the card and trim away the surplus fabric round the edge, so the fabric is about 5 cm (2 in) larger than the card. Keeping the fabric grain straight, push glass-headed pins in along the top edge going through the fabric and right into the edge of the card. Repeat along the lower edge, pulling the fabric gently to tighten it, then repeat along the other 2 sides, folding in the corner fabric neatly.

4 Turn the sampler over. Thread a large needle with string, make a firm knot at the end, then lace the string from top to bottom until you reach the centre. If you run out of string before you reach the centre, join another length with a reef knot. Repeat the lacing in the other direction, then pull the string to tighten the fabric and tie in the centre. Repeat along the remaining 2 sides and frame as desired.

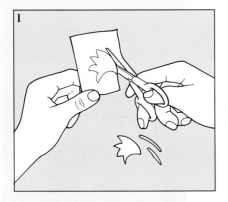

1 *To make a placemat, cut a rectangle of mounting board 33 x 24 cm (13 x 9½ in). Spray paint the mat. Choose four coloured papers in contrasting colours. Refer to the templates on page 164 to cut out two end panels, cutting either a matching pair or one panel freehand. Also cut eight flowers and eight veins or seeds from the papers.*

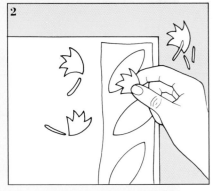

2 *Cut out the cut-outs on the end panels. Arrange the panels within the short ends of the mat. Arrange the flowers between the panels, placing a different coloured stem or pistil with each flower head.*

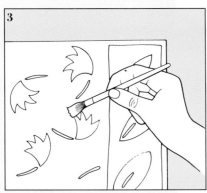

3 *When you are happy with the arrangement, stick all the pieces in place following the gluing technique on page 17. Stick the veins or seeds in the cut-outs. Varnish the mats following the varnishing technique on page 16 using water-based matt varnish.*

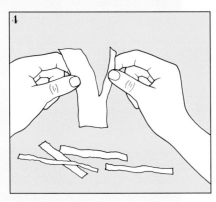

4 *Paint wooden napkin rings with craft paints. Coat both sides of coloured tissue paper with sanding sealer. Tear the tissue into strips when it has dried. Stick the strips in a criss-cross design on the napkin rings following the gluing technique on page 17, sticking the ends inside the ring.*

◀ *These bright and cheery placemats are influenced by floral textiles from the 1930s. A pair of napkin rings patterned with tissue papers continues the theme.*

5 *If the rings have a very curved shape, use short strips and overlap the ends to rejoin them.*

6 *Tear small squares or diamonds of tissue paper and stick in the gaps.*

Home Comforts

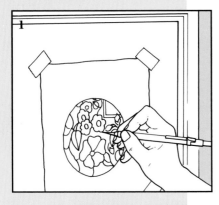

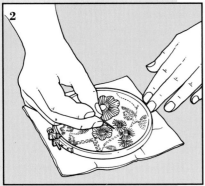

You Will Need
14 mesh plastic canvas
Pale yellow silk dupion
DMC stranded cotton in the following colours: pale yellow 3078 (for needlepoint background), buttercup yellow 973, deep yellow 972; pale pinks 604, 605; mid pink 603, deep pink 602; lavender 211; purple 208; pale blue 3755, mid blue 798; yellow green 703; light blue green 912, mid blue green 911; deep green 909
Tapestry needle size 22
Crewel needle size 7
Small embroidery hoop
Black fine-point felt pen with permanent ink
HB pencil
7.5 cm (3 in), 10 cm (4 in) and 15 cm (6 in) diameter frames

1 *For the free embroidery pictures, trace off the designs on pages 164-165 and transfer them to the fabric as shown pages 98-99, but use a sharp HB pencil instead of an embroidery marker. Leave sufficient space round each motif to mount the fabric in a hoop.*

2 *Using the photograph as a colour guide, embroider the designs using 3 strands of thread in the crewel needle. Work the pink flowers, buds and leaves in long and short stitch (page 26), flower centres in French knots (page 26) and leaf veins in back stitch (page 25). Work the blue flowers in satin stitch (page 26) outlined with back stitch, the stems in back stitch and the purple lines in running stitch (page 24). When all the embroidery is finished, press lightly on the wrong side and mount in the frames following the manufacturer's instructions.*

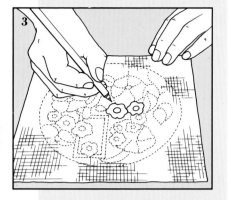

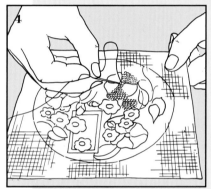

3 *For the needlepoint pictures, trace the designs on pages 164-165 on to paper. Lay the plastic canvas over the tracing and draw over the lines using the black felt pen. To make the work easier to handle, cut away the surplus canvas round the edge, leaving a margin of about 1.5 cm ($^1/_2$ in) all round.*

4 *Using 6 strands of thread in the tapestry needle, work the designs in tent stitch (page 27) using the same colours as the free embroidery pictures. Shade the pink petals towards the centre by using darker shades of pink. Work the flowers, leaves and stems first, then fill in the background in pale yellow thread, stopping just inside the outline. Lay the acetate supplied with the frames over the embroidery to check that the background is large enough to fit the frame. Mount in the frames as above.*

◀ *Make this set of pretty floral pictures as a Christmas gift for a very special friend or relative. Two of the pictures are worked on canvas, while the others are embroidered on pale yellow silk fabric using a variety of free embroidery stitches.*

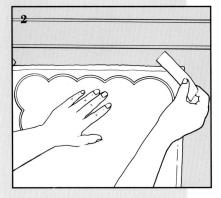

1 *Trace off the napkin motif and scalloped border on page 167 on to paper with the felt pen, repeating the scallop shapes several times as shown to make a border.*

2 *Tape the tracing to a window and secure the square of fabric centrally over the top with strips of masking tape. You should be able to see the traced design through the fabric quite clearly on a bright day - alternatively, use a sheet of glass propped between two dining chairs and direct light upwards from an adjustable table lamp. Draw the design lines on the fabric using the embroidery marker.*

You Will Need

45 cm (17³/₄ in) square of green linen for each napkin
plus 46 x 33 cm (18 x 13 in) for each tablemat
DMC stranded cotton in white (you will need 3 skeins to stitch one napkin and one tablemat)
Crewel needle size 7
Green sewing cotton
Black felt pen with a fine point
Water-soluble embroidery marker
Masking tape

◀ *Stylish yet casual in apple green and white, this design can also be worked in white thread on white linen napkins to grace a formal dinner table.*

3 *Three strands of thread are used for all the embroidery. Begin by working the plain bars which join two edges of the ivy motifs together - work running stitch together — work running stitch (page 24) round the motif until the position for a bar is reached. Strand the thread back and forth 3 times between the motifs, then cover the threads with buttonhole stitch (page 25) and continue the running stitch until the next bar is reached.*

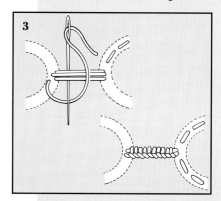

4 *Work branched bars in the same way to join 3 edges of the ivy motifs together, but add a third 'leg' to the stranded threads as shown. Continue working running stitch around the motif. Next, work buttonhole stitch round the ivy shapes, making sure that the looped edge faces outwards. Embroider the leaf veins in back.stitch.*

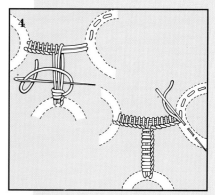

5 *Work 2 rows of running stitch round the scalloped edge, then work buttonhole stitch over the outlines making sure that the looped edge faces outwards. Using small, sharp scissors, cut away the portions of fabric behind the bars. Cut slowly and carefully and take care not to snip into any stitches. Finally, cut away the fabric round the scalloped edge, then rinse in cold water to remove the embroidery marker. Press on the wrong side with a hot iron.*

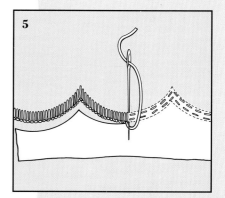

6 *Transfer the tablemat motif on page 167 to one corner of the fabric rectangle and work the cutwork motif in the same way, making sure that the looped edge of the buttonhole stitches outlines the portions of the fabric to be cut away. Turn and pin a narrow hem round the mat and finish off with 2 rows of machine stitching using matching thread, or hem the napkin by hand (page 27). Then rinse the fabric and press.*

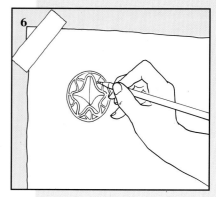

Home Comforts

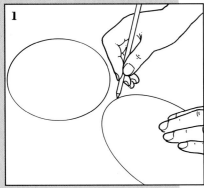

1 *Paint several pictures at the same time on a large piece of silk. Remove the glass or acetate circles from the frames and position them on the silk about 5cm (2in) apart. Carefully draw round each circle and oval with the embroidery marker. Trace off the templates given on pages 164-165, transfer one motif to the centre of each outlined shape.*

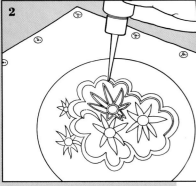

2 *Pin the fabric to the frame using 3-point silk pins. Following the Silk Painting technique on pages 22-23, outline the designs with silver or lilac outliner, working outwards from the centre of the fabric to avoid smudging. Allow the outliner to dry for several hours.*

▶ *A small hand-painted picture would make a wonderful gift for someone special. Here floral designs offer inspiration, but the theme could be animals.*

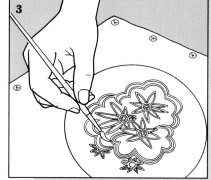

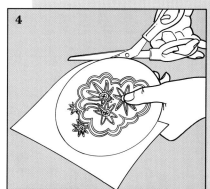

You Will Need:
White 8 Habotai silk
Silk painting frame
Outliner bottle with fine nib
Paintbrushes
Iron-on pelmet interfacing
Fade-away embroidery marker

TULIP PICTURE:
Silver outliner
Silk paints in amethyst, rose
pink, cyclamen pink, reddish
orange, yellowish green, olive
green
Circular wooden frame with 8cm
(3in) aperture

CHRYSANTHEMUM PICTURE:
Lilac outliner
Silk paints in amethyst, ice blue,
orange, pistachio green, olive
green, rose pink, cyclamen,
Bordeaux pink
Circular wooden frame with 10cm
(4in) aperture

BOUQUET WITH BOW:
Silver outliner
Silk paints in amethyst, rose
pink, cyclamen pink, reddish
orange, yellowish green, olive
green
Oval brass frame with 12 x 17cm
(4³⁄₄ x 6³⁄₄in) aperture

TINY FLOWERS:
Lilac outliner
Silk paints in mint green, grass
green, pistachio green, azure
blue, rose pink, carmine red
Circular brass frame with 15cm
(6in) aperture

PINK FLOWERS:
Lilac outliner
Silk paints in grass green,
yellowish green, olive green,
salmon pink, flesh pink,
mandarin yellow, reddish orange
Circular brass frame with 15cm
(6in) aperture

3 Colour in the flower motifs with
a paintbrush, using the
photograph as a colour guide.
Complete all the areas worked in
one colour first and allow to dry.
Fill in the remaining colours one
by one, allowing the paint to dry
between applications. When the
painted silk is completely dry,
remove the silk from the frame,
then fix the colours with an iron
(see page 23), or according to the
manufacturer's instructions.

4 Cut out the circles or ovals,
allowing a margin about 2.5cm
(1in) all round. Back the pieces of
painted silk with interfacing, then
cut out each design, cutting
carefully along the circular or
oval outline. Now following the
manufacturer's instructions, mount
the pieces of silk in their
respective frames.

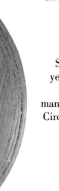

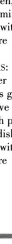

PICTURES AND FRAMES

I F EVERY PICTURE tells a story, then its stencilled frame tells another one! Old pictures and frames are so often designated to the scrap heap, but take a second look at them – they can become individual works of art with a little imagination. The easiest frames to stencil are wide and flat or with a gentle curve. But stencilling does not have to be confined to the frame – a large mount is ideal – or try stencilling the picture.

RIGHT: Old frames can be given a new lease of life with decorative stencilling while smaller pictures can be given additional impact by echoing the motif on the mount.

FRUIT FRAME

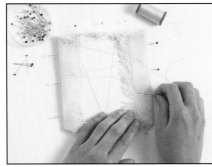

1 *Mount a piece of embroidery with a fruit motif by cutting a piece of white card to the outside measurements of the embroidered area, allowing a border all around. Place the card on the wrong side of the work and fold the excess fabric over the card. Secure by pushing pins into the edge of the card all around. Using a needle and buttonhole thread, secure the embroidery with stitches from top to bottom and from side to side. Oversew to secure and remove the pins. Ask a picture framing service to cut a mount to the measurements of your frame and with a circular aperture. Use the template on page 166 to cut a cherry stencil. With a brush and using gold hard-surface paint, stencil the cherries and three leaves only onto the corners of the mount, masking off the part of the stencil not needed. In red, orange, green and gold paints, stencil the whole motif onto the corners of the frame.*

LEFT: A large mount is very dramatic and leads the eye into the picture. Echo the subject matter subtly in gold stencilling and emphasize the frame edge, rubbing on acrylic gold paint with the tip of your finger.

SILHOUETTES FRAME

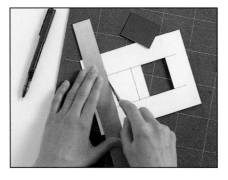

1 *For the mount, measure the recess of the frame and cut dark blue artist's card to this size using a sharp scalpel, a steel rule*

and a cutting board. On the wrong side mark two 4 x 5 cm (1¹/₂ x 2 in) apertures 1.5 cm (¹/₂ in) apart for the silhouettes with a fine marker pen. Cut these openings, finishing the cuts exactly on the marked lines. Cut a piece of white card to the same size as the mount. Lay the mount over the right side of the white card and lightly mark the openings in pencil. Use the templates on page 166 to cut and stencil two silhouettes onto the white card using black paint and a stencil brush (see page 20). To verdigris the metal frame, use a proprietary verdigris mixture and follow the manufacturer's instructions. Replace the mount, add the stencilled silhouettes and the backing board.

FLORAL FRAME

1 Take the backing board off the frame and prepare the wooden surface by sanding thoroughly, then clean the surface to remove dust. Lighten the wood a little with a proprietary wood bleach. Wear rubber gloves and use a glass bowl. Dip a paintbrush in the liquid and paint on sparingly. Leave to dry and re-apply if necessary. Wash off and allow to dry. Cut three stencils from the rose and rosebud templates on page 166. Stencil the motifs onto the frame with a brush (see page 20), using two shades of green, and red, pink and white hard-surface paint. Cut a cardboard mount as for the silhouette frame, making a 5 cm (2 in) square aperture in the centre. Place the mount on large-checked blue fabric, cut 2.5 cm (1 in) larger all around. Trim away the fabric at each corner. Apply general purpose glue to the turnings and press to the wrong side of mount, keeping the fabric taut on the front. Snip into the corners of the central opening and glue the turnings to the mount in the same way.

2 Use the template on page 166 to cut a floral bouquet stencil. Stencil using the brush method in red, yellow and green paints onto the centre of a piece of white card. Cut to the same size as the mount. Fit the fabric mount then the stencilled picture into the frame. Replace the backing board. Moisten the gummed side of 5 cm (2 in) tape with a damp sponge and glue onto the back where the backing board and frame meet. Push the backing board down firmly. Screw in screw eyes with rings on either side of the frame and attach picture wire.

GOOSE FRAME

 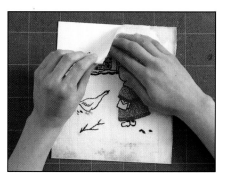

1 This charming embroidery was very badly marked as water, coloured by the wood mount, had stained the fabric. Remove the worst areas of discolouration and any spots with well-diluted household bleach applied on a cotton wool wrapped stick (try a test area first). Lay the embroidery on kitchen paper towel and gently rub with the wet stick. Replace the sticks frequently.

2 Before remounting the embroidery, soak it in a solution of biological washing powder. Lay on kitchen paper towel to dry. Press. Cut a piece of mounting board with an adhesive surface, available from craft stores, on one side to fit the embroidery. Peel off the paper covering and carefully lay the wrong side of the embroidery over the sticky area, starting from one corner and smoothing out any creases. The oak-veneered mount on this picture was badly warped by water. If you have a similar problem, lay the mount on plenty of damp kitchen paper and cover with the same. Cover the entire area of the mount with a large book or similar and pile on a few more to produce a good weight. Leave for several days to dry.

MIRROR

 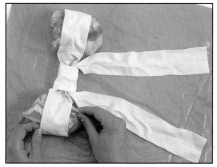

1 Remove the glass from a circular mirror frame approximately 30 cm (12 in) in diameter. Paint using acrylic paint in a copper tone. Replace the mirror. On white cartridge paper and using the oak leaf templates on page 166 to cut stencils, stencil 18 leaves with a stencil brush and acrylic paints in metallic shades of gold, bronze, red and copper. Using small, sharp scissors, cut around each leaf. Use diluted PVA medium to stick in place, overlapping one another and breaking onto the mirror surface. Clean off any glue with a damp cloth.

2 From a 10 cm (4 in) wide strip of cotton fabric cut two pieces 35 cm (14 in) long for tails, one 60 cm (23½ in) length for loops and one 18 cm (7 in) length for a tie. Lay on a surface that can be cleaned. Paint each one on the wrong side with PVA adhesive and fold in the side edges to meet in the centre. Open out a carrier bag and on it place the ends of the loop together. Nip the centre of the circle with the 'tie' and insert the 'tails' under the tie. Support the loops with screwed up plastic bags and leave to dry. Paint with bronze acrylic paint.

ABOVE: Pick out details like flat edges in matching paint. The colour scheme is obviously red and blue. Both are present in the braid, which not only adds a finishing, decorative touch but unites the two colours.

Home Comforts

1 *Prepare the fabric for painting by immersing it in a salt and water solution. Make up a slightly stronger solution than normal using about 5 tablespoons of cooking salt to every half litre of water. Leave the fabric to soak for about ten minutes. Remove the fabric and hang up to drip dry.*

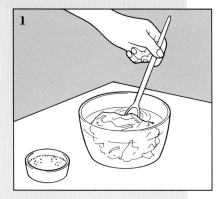

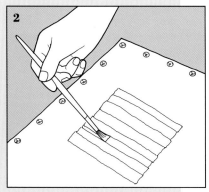

2 *Pin the fabric in the frame using 3-point silk pins. Using a large brush, paint horizontal lines of colour across the fabric, working downwards from the top of the frame. Begin by colouring the sky, painting wide, overlapping stripes of ice blue and opal blue.*

You Will Need:
50cm (20in) square white 8 Habotai silk
Silk painting frame
3-point silk pins
Salt solution
Silk paints in ice blue, opal blue, turquoise, pastel yellow, old gold
Large paintbrush
Fade-away embroidery marker
Black textile marker with fine point
Iron-on pelmet interfacing
Two matching picture frames with 10 x 15cm (4 x 6in) apertures

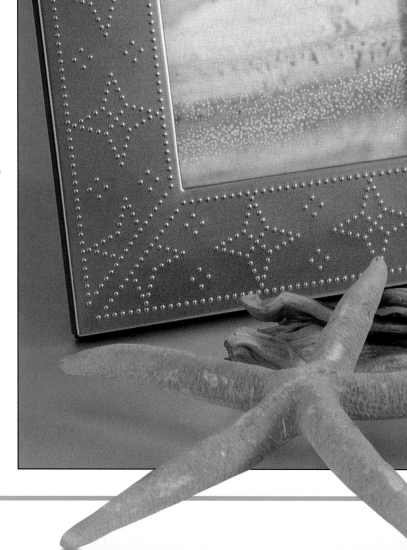

▶ *Salt-treated fabric can be used to make wonderful pictures. A seascape design has been created here, but a sunset would also work well.*

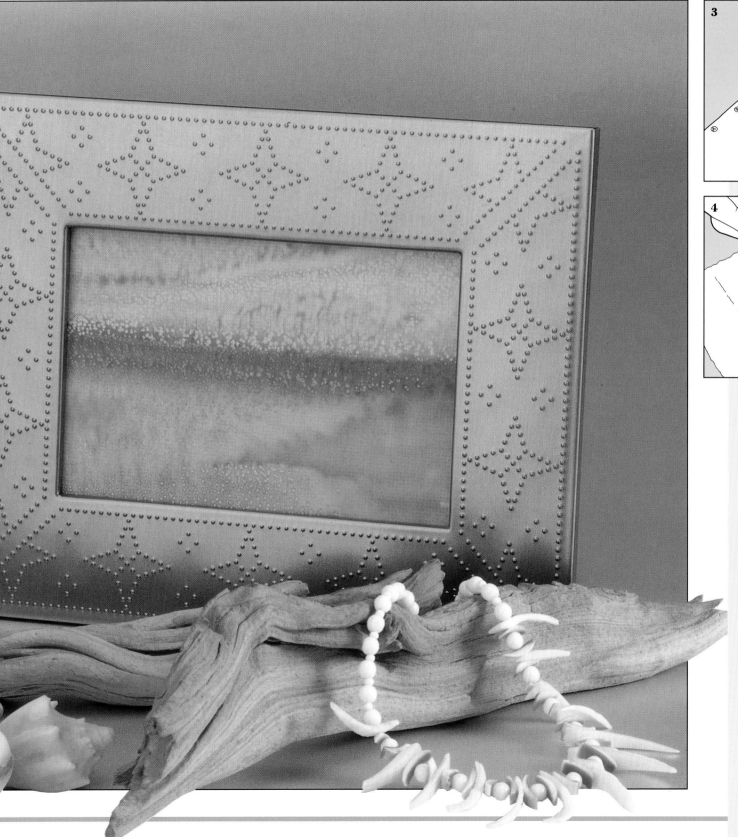

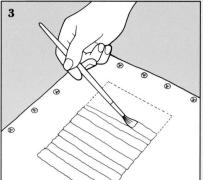

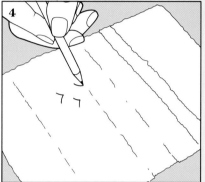

3 *Before the sky dries, paint a narrow stripe of turquoise just below it to make the sea. Allow the paint to dry. For the sand paint wide stripes of pastel yellow below the sea. Quickly, before the pastel yellow dries, add a wide stripe of old gold where the sand meets the sea. Allow to dry, then fix the paint colours.*

4 *Take the backing and glass out of the frames. Place both frames on the painted silk, one vertically and one horizontally, and move them around until you have a pleasing picture showing. Try to have more sky in the vertical frame and more sand in the horizontal frame. Mark the positions with the embroidery marker, remove the frames and cut out, leaving a 2.5cm (1in) margin all round. Back the silk fabric with interfacing, smoothing it as you work. Using a textile marker, draw two or three 'V' shapes in the sky of the vertical picture to represent seagulls, then mount the pictures.*

105

EGYPTIAN BATHROOM

THE BATHROOM is an often neglected room in the house. A sad thought when you consider how much time is spent in there relaxing in a hot bath. It takes very little time to create a peaceful haven – try stencilling on a plain blind or make a fabric shower curtain to hang decoratively outside the plastic waterproof variety. Even tiles can be stencilled successfully with a little help from a can of special varnish!

BELOW: The blue, rag-rolled crenellation represents the Nile, which has plants growing on its banks and water containers waiting to be filled. The sphinxes are instantly recognizable while the flowers are a traditional ancient Egyptian motif.

1 To echo the crenellated edge of the blind illustrated, find the centre and mark lightly with a pencil, then measure out to either side. Calculate the lengths of tape needed to form a channel 2.5 cm (1 in) wide with three evenly spaced crenellations. Run 2.5 cm (1 in) wide masking tape out onto a cutting board, and use its grid lines to cut the tape squarely and accurately. Stick two lines of tape onto the blind forming the channel. Mix up a blue glaze with 50:50 white spirit. Paint and carefully rag roll the area between the tape.

RIGHT: On a large area like the shower curtain spread the motifs out well or you will be there all day stencilling! Do not pay too much attention to the top area of the blind either – most of the time it's rolled up.

2 Cut palm tree, water carrier, flower and sphinx stencils (see page 18) using the templates on page 168. Work the design on the blind using hard surface paints and a stencil brush (see page 20). Use strong shades of red, green, blue and yellow. Complete one half before reversing the stencils for other half. To clean the stencil before turning over, wet kitchen paper towel with cellulose thinners and carefully rub over the paint to dissolve it. Work in a well-ventilated room – the fumes can be unpleasant if inhaled.

3 To calculate the fabric required for the curtain, measure the height of the finished curtain and add 16 cm (6½ in) for turnings. Join widths if necessary. Turn in the selvedges to the wrong side and machine-sew. Along the top, turn down a double 4 cm (1½ in) hem and machine close to the fold. Repeat on the bottom. Count up the number of top rings needed and mark on the curtain top. Working on an old piece of wood with a small hammer, make eyelet holes with a purchased eyelet set. Stencil the curtain with fabric paints to match the blind, using the illustration as a guide.

4 Tiles must be dry and free from any traces of grease or dust before stencilling. Wash down with sugar soap and dry well. Stencil with a stencil brush (see page 20) and hard surface paints in bright colours that are reminiscent of Egyptian designs. To colour in little areas of the stencil, it may be easier to abandon the stencil brush in favour of a stiff artist's brush.

5 Notice that the stencil does not have to be directly centred over the tile – these flowers have been positioned as though growing out of the base of the tile, as they are along the crenellated border on the blind. Protect your hard work with a coat of ceramic varnish, painting over the entire area of the tile.

Wreaths and Garlands

Adorning the home with floral decorations is another way of adding a
personal touch, and this chapter has a host of different ideas
so you can do just that. Wreaths look wonderful simply hanging
on the wall in any room, but they can also bring an interesting accent to a
door. Placed flat, both wreaths and garlands can be used to enhance
a dining table or an entrance way.

Wreaths and Garlands

▲ *This rosehip wreath enhanced with some late blooms on a twisted twig ring makes an attractive end-of-summer decoration with a suggestion of the fruitful season to come.*

You Will Need
Fresh herb foliage such as sage,
purple sage, marjoram,
variegated mint, woodruff
Flowers such as pansies, pinks,
cornflowers, love-in-a-mist,
marigolds, roses,
lady's mantle, feverfew
A double wire ring frame
25 cm (10 in) in diameter
Dry hay or sphagnum moss
Green twine
Silver roll wire
Florists' scissors
Medium-gauge stub wires
Wirecutters

▶ *A heart-shaped wreath of fresh herb flower posies has more than a hint of romance. You can compose the tiny nosegays in advance of a special occasion and keep them in water.*

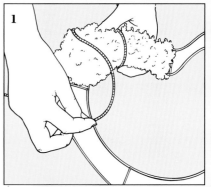

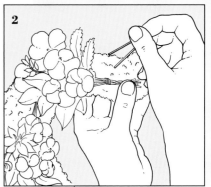

1 Bend the wire frame into a heart shape, pinching it at both ends. Tie the twine to the ring shape. Take small handfuls of the hay or moss and bind them to the frame. Continue until the frame is completely covered with the dry material. Fasten the twine to the frame.

2 Form the foliage and flowers into posies and bind the stem with fine silver wire. Cut stub wires in half and bend them into U-shaped staples. Attach each posy to the frame by pushing a staple over the stems. Bend back the wire ends behind the frame to secure them. Continue around the frame, positioning the posies so that the heads of one cover the stems of the one before.

To keep the fresh-flower decoration looking at its best for as long as possible, spray it frequently with cool water and hang it in a cool airy room away from direct sunlight.

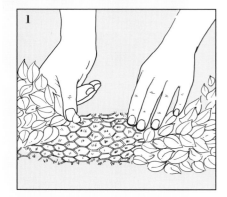

EVENING BUFFET SWAG

1 Make a moss sausage base
following the instructions on
page 14. Cover the swag base
with foliage, using eucalyptus,
senecio and asparagus fern.
2 *Add the white chrysanthemums*
and gypsophila.
3 *Add the feature flowers of*
purple and blue anemones and
freesias. Check that the
arrangement is balanced visually
by concentrating the feature
flowers towards the centre.

▲ *A swag displaying fresh*
flowers makes an attractive
decoration for the front of a
buffet table. Tuck in the stems of
the flowers so that they face
directionally. Make sure that the
flower heads tilt up slightly
towards the top of the swag so
that you can see them from eye
level when the swag is placed in
position on the side of the table.

NAPKIN WITH CUTLERY

1 *Fold the napkin in four to make a square, with the open edges at the top right-hand corner. Take the corner of the top layer of the napkin and fold it to the bottom left-hand corner to make a crease.*

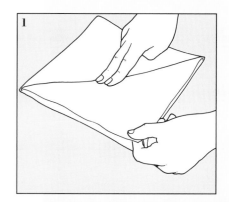

2 *Fold the top layer of the napkin under three times, making the third fold along the crease and leaving a diagonal pocket between the top two layers.*

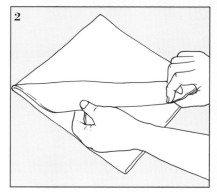

3 *Fold the second layer under twice in the same way. Tuck the edge of this second pocket into the first pocket.*

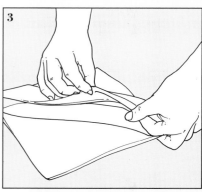

SUGARED ALMOND GIFTBAGS

Net twists of almonds are traditionally given at weddings and christenings, when they should contain one gold almond to bring luck. These giftbags also make pretty table decorations and can be taken home by guests at the end of an evening party. Cut two or three circles of net and place a lacy handkerchief on top of them. Put in the sugared almonds. Secure the handkerchief and net with an elastic band and tie a ribbon in a bow to hide it.

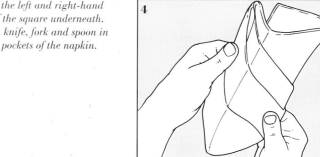

4 *Fold the left and right-hand sides of the square underneath. Place a knife, fork and spoon in the two pockets of the napkin.*

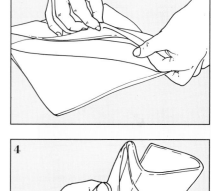

Wreaths and Garlands

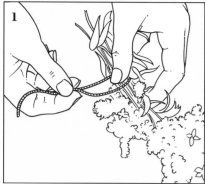

You Will Need
Selection of wayside plant
materials such as rosebay
willowherb, ragwort,
meadowsweet, feverfew,
burdock and thistles
A vine twig ring 30 cm
(12 in) in diameter
Florists' scissors
Green twine

1 *Cut the flowers and seedhead
stems to equal length. Bind three
or four stems of each type into
separate bunches.*

2 *Fasten one end of the twine to
the wreath base, and bind the
bunches onto it so that the heads
of each one cover the stem ends of
the previous one. Continue until
the ring is completely covered.*

▶ *Wild flowers or weeds, call
them what you will, wayside
stems can be used for an outdoor
decoration pretty enough to set
the scene for a party in the
garden.*

Care of Wild Flowers

You may be able to gather wild flowers from your own or a friend's garden. If that is not possible, be sure to cut only rampant weeds from the wayside. It is forbidden to cut all other wild plants.

Many wild flowers are more delicate or more likely to wilt than cultivated forms. Put the stems in water as soon as possible after they have been cut. Bind them into bunches and leave these in water until just before you want to hang the decoration. It takes only a few minutes to bind the bunches onto the ring. Spray the ring with cool water, and do this at frequent intervals if the weather is hot or humid.

115

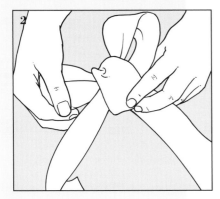

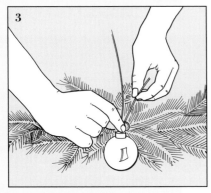

EVERGREEN SWAG

1 *Make a swag base following the instructions on page 14. Cover it with evergreen foliage such as yew or fur, tucking in the stems and working outwards.*

2 *Make two bows using gold wired ribbon. Attach to swag.*

3 *Wire red, gold, bronze and clear tree balls onto the swag.*

DECORATIVE SHAPES

1 *Mix 3 parts plain flour; 3 parts salt to 1½ parts water to a flexible dough. Roll out to 75 mm (¼ in) thick. Cut out Christmas shapes with pastry or biscuit cutters. Pierce a hole at the top of each shape for hanging and at the bottom of the bell shapes to add a 'clapper'. Bake the shapes. Paint the pieces, then varnish them five times to give a high gloss finish.*

2 *Paint details on the bell shapes with gold paint. Hang the shapes on glitter thread, tying the knot just above the hole so that they will hang straight. Glue gold bows to the tops of the bells.*

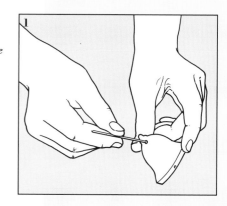

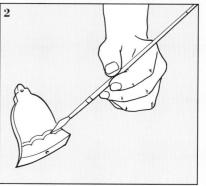

◀ *Bring a festive air to the buffet table by using Christmas baubles and bows to make this evergreen swag. Similar swags can be made for special birthday parties by choosing different colour schemes.*

3 *Push a pipecleaner into a bead. Cut the end about 1 cm (³⁄₈ in) above the bead. Glue the end into the hole at the bottom of the bell.*

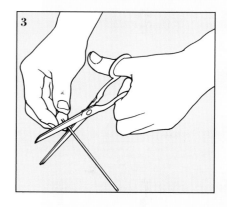

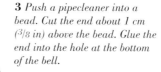

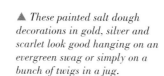

▲ *These painted salt dough decorations in gold, silver and scarlet look good hanging on an evergreen swag or simply on a bunch of twigs in a jug.*

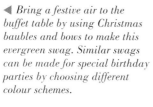

Wreaths and Garlands

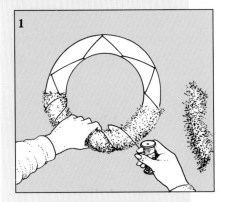

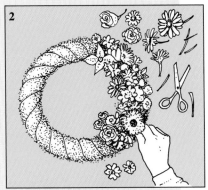

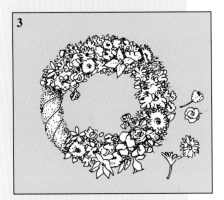

▶ *This garland was made by putting short-stemmed flowers into a damp foam wreath base. It is ideal for fresh flowers, which will last like this for several days. Lots of different species of flower have been combined to colourful effect here, including clematis, marigolds, roses, geraniums, sweet peas, geums and nasturtiums.*

1 *Begin with a wire frame. Wrap moss round the frame and wire it into place with thin rose wire.*

2 *Completely cover the frame with moss, then begin to add flowers and leaves, pushing the stems into the moss. Wire some secure if necessary.*

3 *Continue working right round the frame until it is completely covered with flowers. Spray with a mist of water to keep it fresh.*

◀ *A light and bright summer garland made from daisies, jasmine, feverfew, cornflowers, variegated mint leaves, love-in-a-mist and golden yellow achillea. Strong colours always look fresh if they are mixed with plenty of white for contrast.*

▶ *Full-flowered summer roses are the focus for this beautiful garland. To add to the fragrance, sweet peas are included too, and old-fashioned veronica and astrantia are twinned throughout the circle. It looks lovely on a mellow stone wall, but would look equally good on a door or wall indoors.*

1 *A slightly different approach to making a wreath is first to cover the frame completely with leaves or filler material.*

2 *Add single flowers of the same type at regular intervals right round the frame.*

3 *Finish by filling between main flowers with other small flowers or little bunches of blooms.*

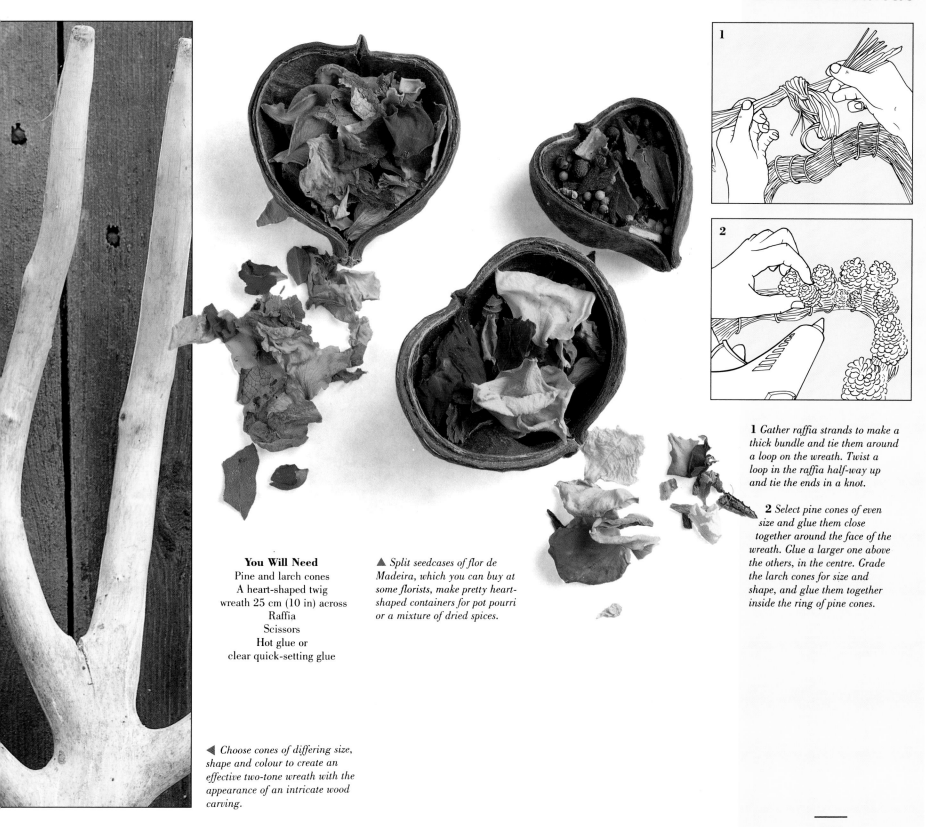

1 *Gather raffia strands to make a thick bundle and tie them around a loop on the wreath. Twist a loop in the raffia half-way up and tie the ends in a knot.*

2 *Select pine cones of even size and glue them close together around the face of the wreath. Glue a larger one above the others, in the centre. Grade the larch cones for size and shape, and glue them together inside the ring of pine cones.*

You Will Need
Pine and larch cones
A heart-shaped twig
wreath 25 cm (10 in) across
Raffia
Scissors
Hot glue or
clear quick-setting glue

▲ *Split seedcases of flor de Madeira, which you can buy at some florists, make pretty heart-shaped containers for pot pourri or a mixture of dried spices.*

◀ *Choose cones of differing size, shape and colour to create an effective two-tone wreath with the appearance of an intricate wood carving.*

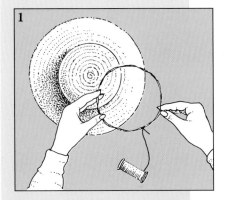

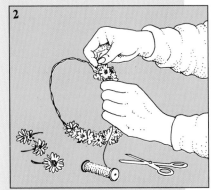

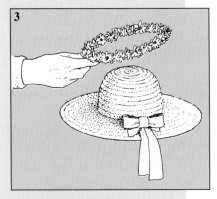

1 *Make a wire circle to fit loosely over the crown of the hat. Twist the ends together and remove from hat.*

2 *Wire short-stemmed flower heads to the circlet, working in one direction right round the circle until you have a wreath of flowers.*

3 *Slide the finished ring over the hat crown and pin or wire it into place. Wire a bow in position to finish off.*

◄ *A child's straw hat makes a perfect base for a pretty dried flower decoration. The flowers can be wired onto a circlet around the crown, or more permanently glued into place. Here the big red bow sets off the bright helichrysums and helipterums, and adds definition and a sense of fun.*

► *A small-scale wreath made from dried flowers. An arrangement like this one can be created using a home-made straw base or a ready-made foam ring. Included in this version are golden yellow helichrysums, achillea flower heads and silvery sea lavender. A little deep brown foliage sets off the light colours well and the silky ribbon adds a lovely finishing touch.*

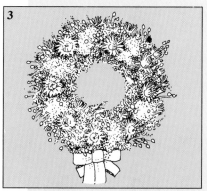

1 You will need a dry foam ring and flower material with stems cut short. Some flowers with soft stems may need to be wired.

2 Begin to cover the foam ring with a base of filler material. Work all around until the ring is covered.

3 Add single flower heads throughout the base covering, keeping the spacing between flowers fairly even and the colours well balanced.

123

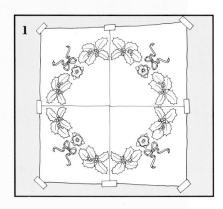

1 *Trace off the design on page 169 4 times using the fine-point felt pen. Stick the 4 tracings together, as shown, to make a large circular design. Secure to a flat surface with strips of masking tape.*

You Will Need
Large piece of thin, closely-woven cream cotton fabric, at least 120 cm (48 in) square
Black textile marker with a fine point
Fabric paint in metallic gold, pearly opaque white, grey green

Glass-headed pins
Strips of thick card
Artist's paintbrushes
Black felt pen with permanent ink
Masking tape
Cream sewing thread

▶ *Surround a Christmas centrepiece complete with festive candle with a cream fabric tablecentre decorated with a hand-painted design in soft green, pearly white and gold.*

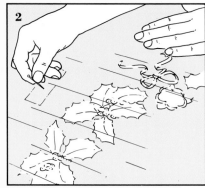

2 *Press the fabric well. Lay it centrally over the traced design and secure with strips of masking tape. To prevent movement round the edges of the design, push fine glass-headed pins through the fabric into the strips of masking tape holding down the tracings.*

3 *Carefully draw the design on the fabric with the textile marker. Work slowly and carefully, going in a clockwise direction if you are right-handed and anti-clockwise if left-handed to avoid smudging the lines. Allow to dry.*

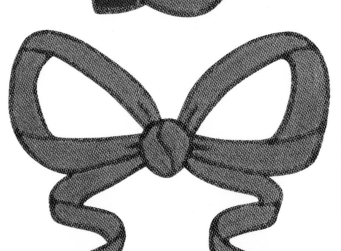

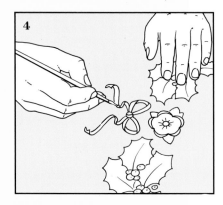

4 *Paint the design (pages 20-21) on the stretched fabric without removing the tracing. Stir the pot of gold fabric paint with a narrow strip of thick card. Using a small brush, fill in the bows, holly berries, flower centres and petal edges with gold paint, working in the same direction as above. Allow to dry – this may take several hours, depending on the temperature of the room.*

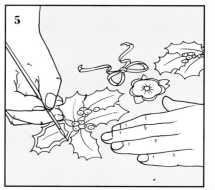

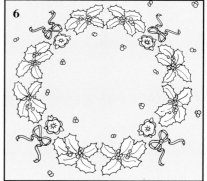

5 *Stirring each pot of paint before application, carefully fill in the flowers with white paint and the leaves with grey green, taking care not to paint over the flower stamens and leaf veins. Make sure you let each colour dry thoroughly before proceeding to the next.*

6 *Finally, use the textile marker to dot tiny groups of holly berries at random over the plain areas of fabric. Fill in the berries with gold paint as above. Fix the painted areas as shown on page 21. Turn a narrow hem round the cloth and secure with a row of machine stitching or hand hemming (page 27) using matching thread.*

Creative Containers

Containers are among the most useful items to have around the home, especially
if they come in a range of sizes. This chapter offers a variety – from bags
and bins which are delightfully decorated with stencils and clever découpage,
to glass bottles highlighted with suns and cherubs, and there's
a perfect set of hat boxes topped with pretty ribbon roses.

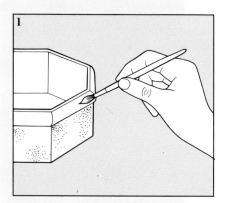

1 *Paint the wooden wine bottle coasters and the bottle box with a layer of emulsion paint thinned with water. Sponge the coasters with gold craft paint, using a light dabbing technique with the sponge. Paint the rims gold. Thin gold craft paint with water and use it to paint the edges of the bottle box.*

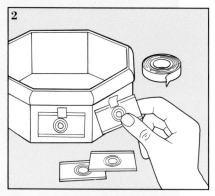

2 *For the coasters, cut out motifs from giftwrap. Refer to the arranging motifs technique on page 17 to position the motifs on the coasters. Wide strips of giftwrap were cut into sections and positioned on each hexagonal side. A head or glove motif and a narrow strip were applied to each hexagonal side of the green coaster.*

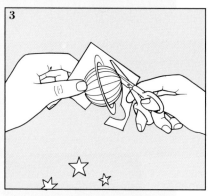

3 *Cut out motifs from giftwrap for the bottle box. Place the bottles in the box and arrange the motifs where they will be visible between the bottles and on the front and sides of the box. Stick in place with masking tape. Place small stars at random in any small gaps. Remove the bottles.*

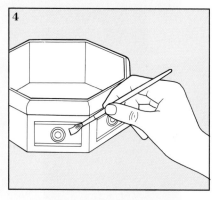

4 *Glue and varnish the pieces with water-based satin varnish following the gluing and varnishing techniques on pages 16-17. The bottle box was crackle glazed, then gold wax, available at art stores, was lightly rubbed into the cracks.*

▶ *Mythical gods and a galaxy of stars and planets decorate a bottle box and wine bottle coasters. The rich colours are highlighted with touches of gold.*

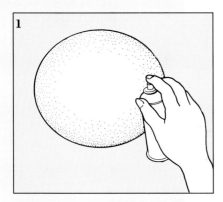

1 *Refer to the instructions on page 24 to make a large, round box and lid. Use deep pink paper to cover the box and lid. Spray the lower half of the box side, lid rim and circumference of the circle for the lid with blue spray paint.*

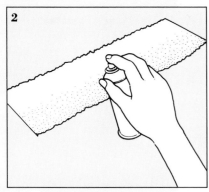

2 *Make 4 flower centres: bend a wire stem into a hook and wrap with a ball of cotton wool Glue a 4 cm (1½ in) diameter of green crepe paper over the ball. Glue a fringed strip of green crepe paper around two flower centres, the ends cut to points. Cut 8 cm (3¼in) wide strips of pink, deep pink and mauve crepe paper, and spray the long, lower edges with blue paint. Use the template on page 169 to cut 6 pink, 6 deep pink and 12 mauve petals from crepe paper. Stretch the petals widthways.*

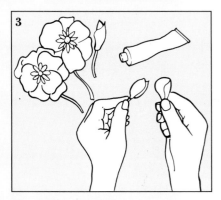

3 *Glue 3 pink petals then 3 deep pink petals and finally 4 mauve petals to each fringed flower centre. To make buds, glue a mauve petal around each of the remaining flower centres, then glue a second mauve petal around the first on each bud.*

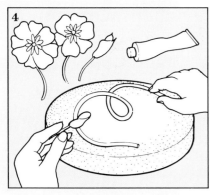

4 *Bind narrow strips of green paper ribbon around the flower and bud stems. Cut a 45 cm (18 in) length of coiled green paper ribbon. Arrange on the box lid with the flowers and buds. Glue the flowers and buds in position, then the paper ribbon.*

▲ These round boxes are both attractive and practical. Make a range in different papers and sizes to hold treasured letters, keepsakes or items of jewellery.

◄ Have fun experimenting with colourful crepe papers to make alternative fantasy-style flowers in various sizes, shapes and hues.

1 *Follow the instructions on page 24 to make a large, round box and a lid covered with striped paper. Cut 2 strips of crepe paper 4 cm (1½in) wide and one strip 7.5 cm (3 in) wide. Cut the paper with the ends parallel with the grain of paper. Spray the long edges lightly with spray paint. Stretch the long edges between thumb and forefinger.*

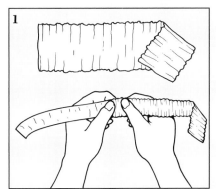

2 *Place the narrow strips across the top of the lid and secure the ends inside on the underside of the lid with double-sided adhesive tape. To make the bow, trim one wide strip to 35 cm (14 in) in length. Fold the ends into the centre. Make concertina pleats widthways at the centre.*

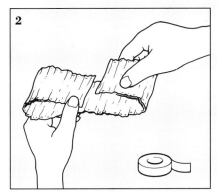

3 *Cut the remaining wide strip 17 cm (7 in) long. Fold in concertina pleats across the centre. Hold the strip against the back of the bow, matching centres, and bind together with a narrow strip of crepe paper. Glue the ends at the back of the bow.*

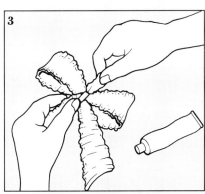

4 *Trim the bow 'tails' into a fishtail shape. Glue the bow to the narrow crepe paper strip on the lid. The photograph also shows a small, round box covered with giftwrap; made by following the instructions on page 24, but using scaled down measurements.*

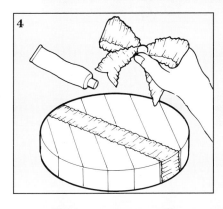

Creative Containers

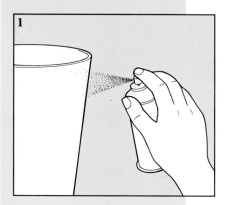

1 *Spray paint the waste bin with cream-coloured paint. Lightly spray the heraldic waste bin with mustard and yellow paint. Lightly spray the clock waste bin with silver and blue paint. Tear coloured tissue into irregular squares and rectangles. To strengthen the tissue, apply a coat of sanding sealer to both sides.*

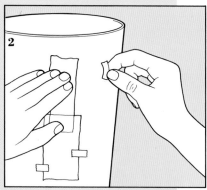

2 *Arrange the tissue pieces on the waste bins, overlapping the colour and sticking lightly in place with masking tape. Stick the tissue pieces in position following the gluing technique on page 17.*

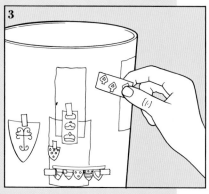

3 *Cut motifs from giftwrap. Heraldic shields, crowns and historic symbols were used for the heraldic waste bin – cut some of the motifs out neatly and others into an uneven square or rectangle. Clock faces were cut from giftwrap for the clock waste bin. Clock faces cut from magazine advertisements will also look very effective. Arrange the motifs on the waste bin, sticking them on lightly with masking tape.*

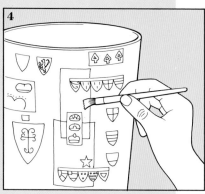

4 *When you are happy with the design, stick the pieces in position following the gluing technique on page 17. Varnish the waste bins following the varnishing technique on page 16 and using water-based matt varnish.*

▶ *Revamp old waste bins with spray paints, fine tissue papers and delicate paper motifs.*

Creative Containers

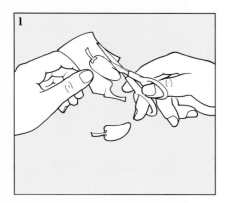

1 *Thin yellow and apricot craft paints with water on a ceramic tile or old plate. Using a brush, paint a small chest blending the colours together as you work. Cut out motifs from giftwrap or magazines. Photographic images of foods and flowers were used to decorate this chest.*

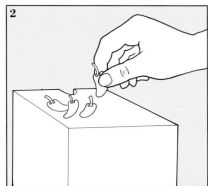

2 *With the drawer fronts uppermost, arrange the motifs on the fronts, grouping together similar images on each drawer.*

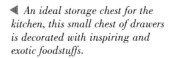

◀ *An ideal storage chest for the kitchen, this small chest of drawers is decorated with inspiring and exotic foodstuffs.*

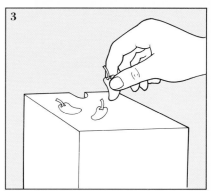

3 *Following the gluing technique on page 17, stick the motifs in place. Stick single images such as large flower heads to the top and sides of the chest.*

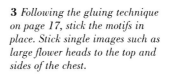

4 *Varnish the decorated chest with water-based satin varnish following the varnishing technique shown on page 16. You need apply only one coat of varnish to the sides of the drawers.*

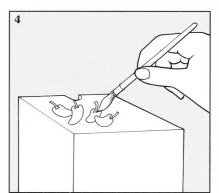

QUILL AND PEN STATIONERY SET

LETTER WRITING is still the most enduring form of communication, and all the more pleasurable if you have elegant accessories to use! Old letter racks, index files and blotters are easily found and can be renovated in subtle antique tones for the study, or in strong, eye-catching colours for the home office. Keep bills tidy, store family photographs and keep favourite magazine recipes in order with this attractive set of stationery items.

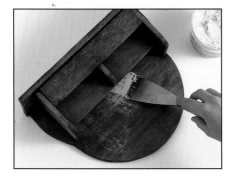

INDEX FILE

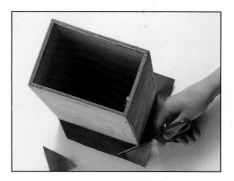

1 Remove the drawer from the box. Using a screwdriver with a fine head, carefully pull up the handle – this one was plastic – taking care not to damage the surface. Replace this with a brass handle or card carrier on completion.

2 This index file was made from a mixture of wood and thick cardboard. A wallpaper stripping agent will remove the paper from both if care is taken not to soak the cardboard too much. Once the liquid has soaked through the paper layer, gently prize it off with a metal scraper. Try to memorize the order of any overlaps or joins on the original paper.

3 Allow to dry thoroughly before covering with new paper. Select a good quality, plain one. Starting with the back of the box, cut the paper to fit, leaving 2 cm (¾ in) overlap all around. Paste the wrong side with PVA medium, press in place and trim the excess off the corners. Stick the overlapping paper to the sides. Cover the body of the box and the drawer in the same way and leave to dry. Use the templates on page 170 to cut a quill and pen motif and two small oak leaf stencils (see page 18). Stencil with a brush (see page 20) in red, green, navy, black and gold hard-surface paints. Mask off the oak leaf design around the pen and quill when stencilling these to prevent colours from accidentally mixing.

LETTER RACK

BLOTTER

1 Remove the varnish with a paint stripper, and decide on the final finish you want. If the wood has a beautiful grain it would be a shame to paint it, but it is better to paint it if it is damaged. Fill any holes and scratches with a fine surface filler, using a metal filler knife. Sand the surface smooth when the filler is dry.

2 The base feet and the original thirties plastic feet on this letter rack were replaced. Where possible, use the original screw holes, drilling holes to match in the new base piece. Tiny wooden door handles were used as replacement feet. Stick in place with wood glue. Apply two coats of eggshell in two shades of blue. In a well-ventilated room, clean the stencils cut for the index file with cellulose thinner. Stencil the motifs onto the letter rack as described for the index file.

1 Gilding is a wonderful method of creating instant age and makes a very ordinary object look expensive. Purchase red fontenay paste, gilt cream and optional gilt patina pencils from good art stores. Prepare the surface of an old blotter to reveal bare wood by stripping or sanding off old paint or varnish. Paint the handle and top of the blotter with fontenay paste. Allow to dry Paint the curved underpart with two coats of blue eggshell. Leave to dry.

2 Paint over the red fontenay paste with gilt cream, using a stiffish brush. Dry, then sand off gently in places with fine grade wire wool to reveal the red layer beneath. With a clean cloth, buff to a soft sheen. The object can be left like this or more ageing and highlights added with patina pencils. Crayon them on in tiny lines or in small areas. Refer to step 3 of the index file to decorate the curved underpart of the blotter by stencilling with the small oak leaf motifs.

CANDLESTICKS

1 *The original finish on these candlesticks was so fine they only needed a light rub with medium grade wire wool to give a 'key' for the paint. Wrap the steel wool around an area and rotate the candlestick within it, to create a smooth surface. Finish with fine grade wool and paint with two coats of blue eggshell. The metal areas were painted in copper, an artist's brush being dipped into a small amount of paint sprayed into the lid of the can. Clean brushes in white spirit.*

ABOVE: Adapt a space under the stairs or display stationery items in a corner to show them to their best advantage. They will look particularly attractive arranged on natural wood in dark, rich colours. The candlesticks can also be used as table centrepieces or to decorate a mantelpiece.

LEFT: An index file was used to list names and addresses chronologically, but now its uses are endless. Classify a compact disc collection, notes on the family tree or just store odds and ends in it!

2 *To unify the metal and wood and create an up-to-the-minute look, try a verdigris effect on the metal. Verdigris is traditionally done in shades of green, but can also be worked in shades of blue. Verdigris pastes can be bought in either colour. When working with the verdigris paste, try not to get it on to the blue paintwork. Sand carefully with fine wire wool to reveal the copper paint. Position the small oak leaf stencils (also used on the index file) on the areas you want to decorate and stencil as before.*

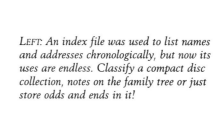

Creative Containers

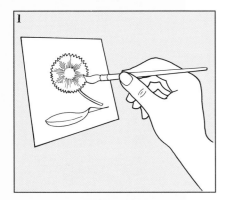

1 *To decorate the large green cup and saucer, photocopy botanical motifs from copyright-free source books, available from art and craft stores, onto coloured paper. Apply sanding sealer to both sides of the paper to protect the surface. Cut out the motifs, cutting off any fine details such as stems as these can be painted on later.*

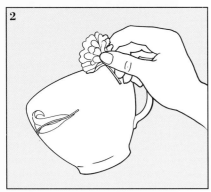

2 *Arrange the motifs on the cup and saucer and stick them lightly in place with masking tape. Refer to the gluing technique on page 17 to stick the pieces to the china, making cuts into the motif so that they lie flat over the curved surface. Paint in the fine details using ceramic paint.*

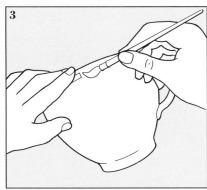

3 *To decorate the yellow mosaic cup and saucer, cut green and black coloured paper into strips approximately 8 mm (5/16 in) wide. Cut the strips into squares and rectangles. Apply PVA medium to the top of a section of the cup and press green rectangles in a row onto the PVA medium. Continue sticking on the rectangles around the cup, wiping away the excess glue with a damp kitchen towel as you work.*

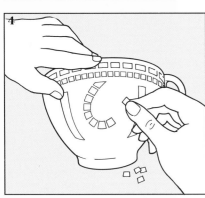

4 *Add a row of black squares below the green rectangles. Decorate the outer edge of the saucer in the same way. Measure the circumference of the cup with a tape measure and divide the cup into fifths with masking tape. Arrange black squares in a spiral design within one section. Stick in place with PVA medium, trimming the first and last square diagonally. Decorate the other sections in the same way. Remove the masking tape and glue a green square between each spiral.*

5 *Cut five 2 cm (¾ in) diameter circles of paper for templates and arrange equidistantly apart on the saucer. Stick black squares around each circle with PVA medium. Remove the templates. Stick a green square between each circle.*

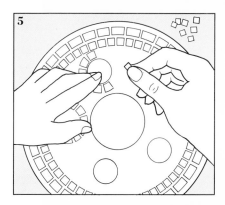

6 *To cover a small cup and saucer completely, cut out lots of 3 cm (1¼ in) diameter circles of green patterned giftwrap and magazine pictures. Stick the circles to the cup and saucer following the gluing technique on page 17, overlapping the circle edges so that the china is completely covered. Cut into the circles so that the paper lays flat.*

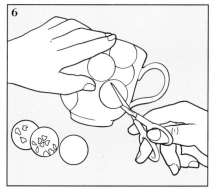

7 *Cut out cup shapes from yellow patterned paper giftwrap and magazine pictures. Stick around the cup and saucer.*

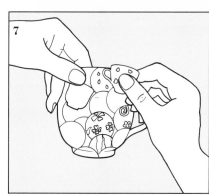

8 *Varnish the cups and saucers with water-based satin varnish following the varnishing technique on page 16.*

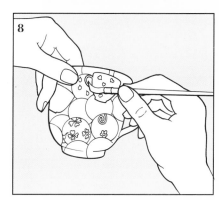

◄ *Découpaged cups and saucers will have pride of place in a pretty kitchen. Here are three different methods of decorating chinaware.*

Creative Containers

1 *Use a pair of pliers to remove the wire handle from a metal bucket. Spray paint the bucket and a metal watering can in bright colours.*

2 *To decorate the watering can, cut out flower heads from giftwrap. Sunflowers have been used in this example. Arrange the flowers around the watering can following the arranging motifs technique on page 17. Stick the flowers in place following the gluing technique on page 17. Stick one flower to the top of the can. Use a hole punch to punch holes in a co-ordinating coloured paper. Glue the punched circles in a border around the watering can and along the handle.*

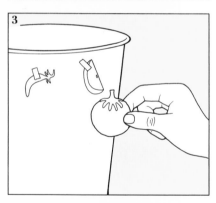

3 *To decorate the bucket, cut out gardening motifs from giftwrap. Arrange the pieces on the bucket at random following the arranging motifs technique on page 17. Stick down following the gluing technique on page 17.*

4 *Paint the bucket rim in a contrasting colour with enamel paint. Varnish the watering can and bucket with water-based gloss varnish following the varnishing technique on page 16. Paint the wooden handle for the bucket, then replace on the bucket.*

Creative
Containers

◀ *This colourful metal bucket and watering can, decorated with gardening motifs, would make a cheery addition to a conservatory.*

141

Creative Containers

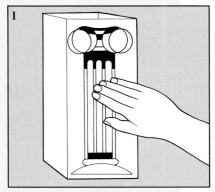

1 *To decorate the tall red vase, cut one motif from giftwrap large enough to fit the length of the vase – the ancient architectural column shown here was perfect. Stick in place following the gluing technique on page 17.*

2 *Drape some floral motifs cut from giftwrap around the column and lightly stick in place with masking tape. Glue in position. Glue various motifs to the other glass vessels. Varnish the glassware with water-based gloss varnish following the varnishing technique on page 16.*

Plain coloured glassware can be transformed into designer-style pieces with the application of various paper motifs.

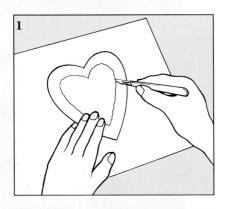

1 *Using the template on page 170, cut out a large heart for the base from thick handmade paper. Also cut a heart for the lid adding 1 mm (¹/₁₆ in) to the circumference. Cut out the inside of the heart lid along the wavy line.*

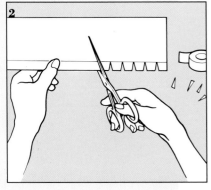

2 *Refer to the diagram on page 172 to cut out the large heart box side and rim. Cut a wavy edge along the lower edge of the rim. Score along the broken lines on the wrong side and bend the tabs forwards at right angles. Apply double-sided adhesive tape to the tabs on the right side, then snip the lower and upper tabs to the scored line at 7 mm (⁵/₁₆ in) intervals.*

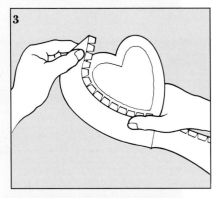

3 *With the point of the heart matched to the centre fold, attach the lower tabs of the box side to the base and the upper tabs of the rim to the underside of the lid. With both the box side and the rim, stick the end tabs under the opposite ends.*

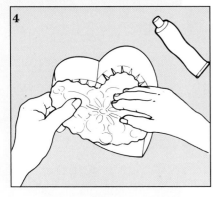

4 *Paint a doily in a coordinating colour. Leave to dry, then cut a heart to fit inside the lid. Glue to the underside of the lid so that the doily pattern fills the cut-out heart on the lid. Fill the box with pot pourri.*

◀ The fine filigree on the lid of this heart-shaped, subtly-coloured box filled with pot pourri allows the heady fragrance to filter into the atmosphere of your home.

▲ These two miniature heart-shaped boxes are ideal for storing rings, cuff-links or earrings – or for presenting precious gifts.

1 Use thick paper for the boxes or apply giftwrap to thin card with spray glue. For the bases, cut out 2 small hearts using the template on page 170. Also cut out 2 hearts for the lids, adding 1 mm ($^1/_{16}$ in) to the circumference in each case. For the beaded box lid, cut out a tiny heart along the solid lines using the template on page 170. Score along the broken line and lift each side upwards. Glue a piece of contrasting paper on the reverse of each half of the heart.

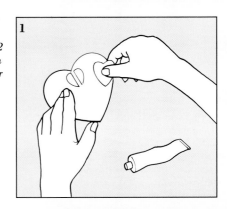

2 Refer to the diagram on page 172 to cut out 2 small heart box sides and rims. Score along the broken lines on the wrong side and bend the tabs forwards at right angles. Apply double-sided adhesive tape to the tabs on the right side, then snip the lower and upper tabs to the scored lines at 7 mm ($^5/_{16}$ in) intervals.

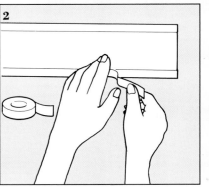

3 Matching the points of the hearts to the centre folds, attach the lower tabs of the boxes' sides to the bases and the upper tabs of the rims to the undersides of the lids. Stick the end tabs under the opposite ends. Carefully glue sequins and small beads to the tiny heart of the beaded box, then at random to the lid.

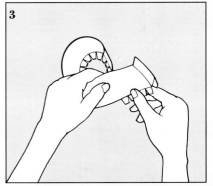

4 Alternatively, make a dragonfly for the box lid. Using the template on page 156, cut a body from reptile skin effect paper and an upper and lower wing from green card and iridescent film. Attach each wing to a card wing at the centre with double-sided adhesive tape. Glue the wings together and the body centrally on top. Use a piece of adhesive foam to attach the dragonfly to the box lid.

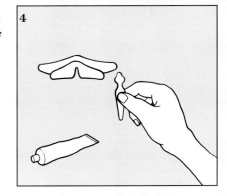

FARMHOUSE KITCHENWARE

OLD FASHIONED enamelware is making a comeback in the kitchen. Copies of 1950s designs can be bought again, while original pieces can be found at flea markets and second-hand stores. These are often dented or chipped and are not to be recommended for use in the preparation of food. However, they are wonderful stencilled as decorative pieces out on display. Match them up with other items to give total co-ordination.

SCALES

1 The weighing bowl on this basic set of scales was made from tin. Much better looking are brass or copper bowls. Cheat a little and colour the bowl with brass, copper or bronze spray paint in a can. This bowl was painted brass to match the lovely brass weights that were bought with it. Two iron weights that were also part of the set were given several coats of blackboard paint before being stencilled to match the scales.

HERB DRAWERS

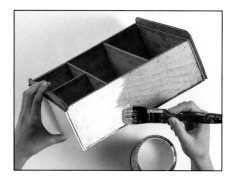

1 Create a set of herb drawers from an old miniature chest. This one, though crudely made from cheap timber, had good proportions and lovely china handles. These were carefully unscrewed and the old paint cleaned off with fine wire wool and paint stripper. Use rubber gloves if you can, or coat your hands with barrier cream to protect them. Strip off the old finish and sand smooth with fine sandpaper. The entire surface need not be painted as a little natural wood showing adds to the country feel. Cover the areas to be painted with acrylic primer, masking the edges if necessary. Acrylic primer dries quickly, making handling easier when the whole object is not being painted. Cover the primed areas with pale green eggshell paint. Allow to dry. Remove masking tape.

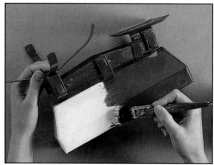

2 Paint the base of the scales with red oxide metal primer (an awkward shape like these scales may need two coats to cover all the nooks and crannies). Then coat in a rich cream oil-based paint such as eggshell. Painting such a pale colour over the dark metal primer will require several coats. Dry well between coats.

RIGHT: Once no longer in use, old coffee and teapots make ideal objects for decorating with stencilling and displaying in a kitchen cabinet or on a dresser.

RIGHT: *Old kitchenware often has particularly appealing shapes. You will probably have some old kitchenware yourself in your attic or storeroom*

BELOW: *Pick items with varying shapes and heights to make an interesting display of kitchenware. These charming pieces, gathered from a variety of sources, are painted in clotted cream and herb shades and decorated with appropriate country images to fit the style and atmosphere of the kitchen decorated in farmhouse style.*

TEAPOT AND COFFEEPOT

1 Even badly stained enamel, as often found in old teapots, can be cleaned effectively. Soak in a bowl of cold water and biological washing powder. Leave for a couple of days if necessary and scrub intermittantly with a pan scourer which will not scratch the surface.

2 Fill any chips or dents with two-part car filler, available from car accessory stores, following the manufacturer's directions for use. Any rust should be treated with a rust removal product. Paint the object inside and out with red oxide metal primer. In damp weather, the inside may take several days to dry. Paint on several coats of green or cream eggshell paint. Allow each coat to dry thoroughly before painting the next.

STENCILLING

1 Use the templates on page 171 to cut stencils of the floral and cow motifs (see page 18). Stencil onto the tea and coffee pot base and lid, the base of the scales and iron weights and onto the front of each herb drawer. Stencil with a brush (see page 20) in soft shades of green, pink, blue and brown hard-surface paints. Use spray adhesive and masking tape to keep the stencils in place. Pick out any details on the pots using one of the stencilling colours and an artist's paint brush to colour knobs and rims. To age your kitchenware, try crackling it, using one of the varieties of crackling varnish available from good paint and art stores. Follow the manufacturer's directions carefully.

2 When the crackling is quite dry, make up an ageing solution to patinate or darken the cracks. Mix some artist's oil paint in a burnt umber shade with a little white spirit to the consistency of double or heavy cream. Paint it all over – do not worry if it looks like a dreadful mistake. Allow to dry for a few minutes before wiping off the excess with a clean rag. Leave the paint in the cracks to dry. The entire surface of your kitchenware will be slightly darkend by using this treatment.

Creative Containers

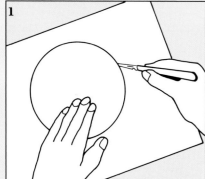

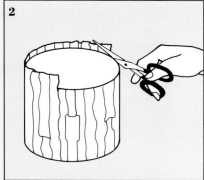

1 *To make the round jardinière, cut a circle 17 cm (6¾ in) in diameter from corrugated card for the base and a strip of thin card 60 x 15 cm (24 x 6 in). For the oval jardinière, cut an oval of corrugated card 25 cm (10 in) long and 20 cm (8 in) wide for the base and a strip of thin card 85 x 17 cm (33½ x 6¾ in). Attach the strips to their bases, sticking the card together with brown tape.*

2 *Apply ten layers of papier mâché to the jardinières following the layered method on page 18, extending the newspaper strips above the upper edges. Trim the upper edges level with the card. Carefully sand and undercoat the jardinière.*

▶ *These elegant stencilled jardinières are based on traditional papier-mâché designs. Interesting and attractive tortoiseshell and malachite effects can be achieved by simply sponging on paint.*

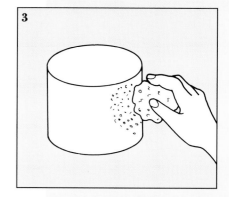

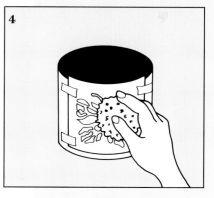

3 Use craft paint to apply a base colour to the outside of the jardinières – here, ochre was used for the round jardinière, green for the oval. Using a paintbrush, apply a thin film of paint to an old plate. Dab at the paint with a damp natural sponge, then dab the sponge over the base colour. The round jardinière was sponged with brick red, brown and black paint. A copper colour was sponged onto the oval jardinière.

4 Paint the inside and rim of both jardinières – black was used for the round jardinière and copper for the oval. Use the templates on page 170 to trace the swag or butterfly onto stencil card. Cut away the cut-out areas and attach the stencil to the front of the jardinière with masking tape. Using a natural sponge, dab paint through the cut-out areas onto the jardinière. Varnish the jardinières with polyurethane varnish when the paint has dried.

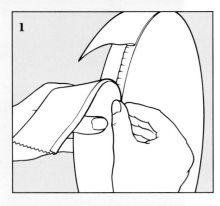

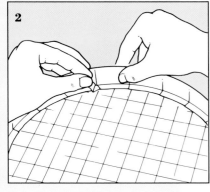

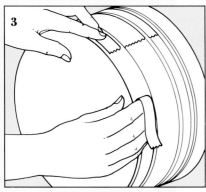

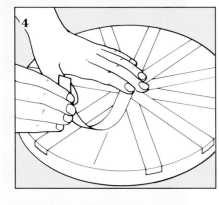

Measurements for ribbon amounts given are based on a hatbox with a circumference of 90 cm (35¹/2 in), a depth of 14.5 cm (5³/4 in) deep and with lid sides 3 cm (1¹/5 in) deep.

1 *Use pinking shears to cut ribbon and fabric. From a 60 x 92 cm (23¹/2 x 37 in) length of white moiré taffeta, cut and stick a 17 x 92 cm (6³/4 x 36¹/4 in) rectangle around the hatbox sides. Fold the top edge inside and the lower edge underneath the hatbox. From a 45 x 92 cm (18 x 36¹/4 in) piece of thin white card cut and stick a 27.5 cm (10⁴/5 in) diameter circle onto the base and another to the inside. Line the inside with 14 x 92 cm (5¹/2 x 36¹/4 in) of card. Cover the lid top with a 30 cm (12 in) diameter moiré taffeta circle, snipping and sticking excess fabric to the sides. Press 1 cm (²/5 in) to the wrong side along one long edge of an 8 x 92 cm (3¹/5 x 36¹/4 in) strip of moiré taffeta. Stick to the lid rim with the fold along the top edge.*

2 *Fold and stick the lower edge of the strip to the inside of the lid, snipping where necessary. Line the lid with a 28 cm (11 in) diameter card circle.*

3 *With the lid on, use a vanishing marking pen to mark the ribbon width positions so they are evenly spaced between the lid rim and bottom of the base. Cut a 92 cm (36¹/4 in) length of pale pink 50 mm (2 in) wide single satin ribbon and cut a 184 cm (72¹/2 in) length of 23 mm (⁹/10 in) wide deep pink single satin in half. Use spray adhesive to stick the ribbon around the hatbox.*

4 *With the vanishing marking pen, draw a six-line star on the lid. Cut six 31 cm (12²/5 in) lengths from 3.7 m (4 yd 2 in) of 23 mm (⁹/10 in) wide pale pink single satin ribbon. Stick the ribbon over the lines, sticking the ends flat against the sides.*

5 *Stick 184 cm (72¹/₂ in) of 23 mm (⁹/₁₀ in) wide pale pink single satin ribbon twice around the lid rim.*

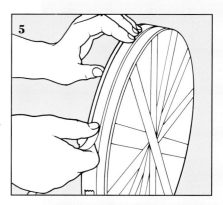

6 *Make seven square roses using 4.2 m (4¹/₂ yd) of 22 mm (⁴/₅ in) wide deep pink double satin ribbon, folding at right angles. Use strong glue to stick a ring of six roses around a central rose on the lid.*

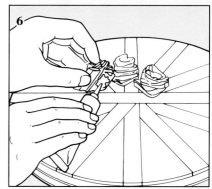

1 *Mark a line 3 cm (1¹/₅ in) up from the base around the hatbox. Stick 92 cm (36¹/₄ in) of 75 mm (3 in) wide deep pink double satin ribbon around the hatbox above this line. Mark points opposite each other about 13 cm (5¹/₁₀ in) apart along both ribbon edges. Cut 2.86 m (3 yd 6¹/₂ in) of 13 mm (¹/₂in) wide pale pink single satin ribbon into 11 cm (4¹/₂ in) lengths. Centring ribbon ends over the marks, stick lengths diagonally in one direction across the wide ribbon and then in the opposite direction. Cut the ends level with the wide ribbon edges. Cut two 92 cm (36¹/₄ in) lengths of 10 mm (²/₅ in) wide deep pink single satin ribbon. Stick over the latticed ribbon ends along each edge of the wide ribbon.*

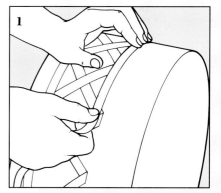

2 *Stick 184 cm (72¹/₂ in) of 23 mm (⁹/₁₀ in) wide pale pink satin ribbon twice around the rim. Cut 2.88 m (3 yd 4¹/₂ in) of 36 mm (1²/₅ in) wide dark pink satin ribbon into 9 lengths. Sew length ends together to form a ring. Gather one edge to make a rossette. Cover 9 buttons (see page 23) sew to the rossette centres. Stick in a circle on the lid. Make a double rossette in the same way, gathering together one ring of 50 cm (20 in) of 73 mm (3 in), wide deep pink double satin ribbon, and another ring of 40 cm (15³/₄ in) of 50 mm (2 in) wide pale pink double satin ribbon. Add a 25 mm (1 in) button covered with pale pink ribbon and stick to the lid.*

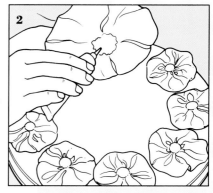

CLASSIC MOTIF ONE
Same size (Cut 1)

CLASSIC RUG
Pages 30-31

CLASSIC MOTIF TWO
Same size (Cut 1)

Templates

The following pages present the templates, diagrams and charts for the projects. The diagrams are constructed from measurements. Use a ruler and set square to draw the pieces onto card to use as a template. It is important to follow either the metric or imperial measurements, but not a combination of both.

Some templates are reduced in size where stated. Enlarge the templates on a photocopier by the percentage given.

To make a complete pattern for symmetrical shapes, place the pattern on a piece of folded paper matching the 'place to fold' line to the folded edge. Cut out and open the pattern flat to use.

Embroider one stitch on the fabric for every coloured square shown on the charts.

IVY-LEAF TIE-BACK
Page 42

LEAF AND BERRIES
Enlarge by 150%
(Cut 1)

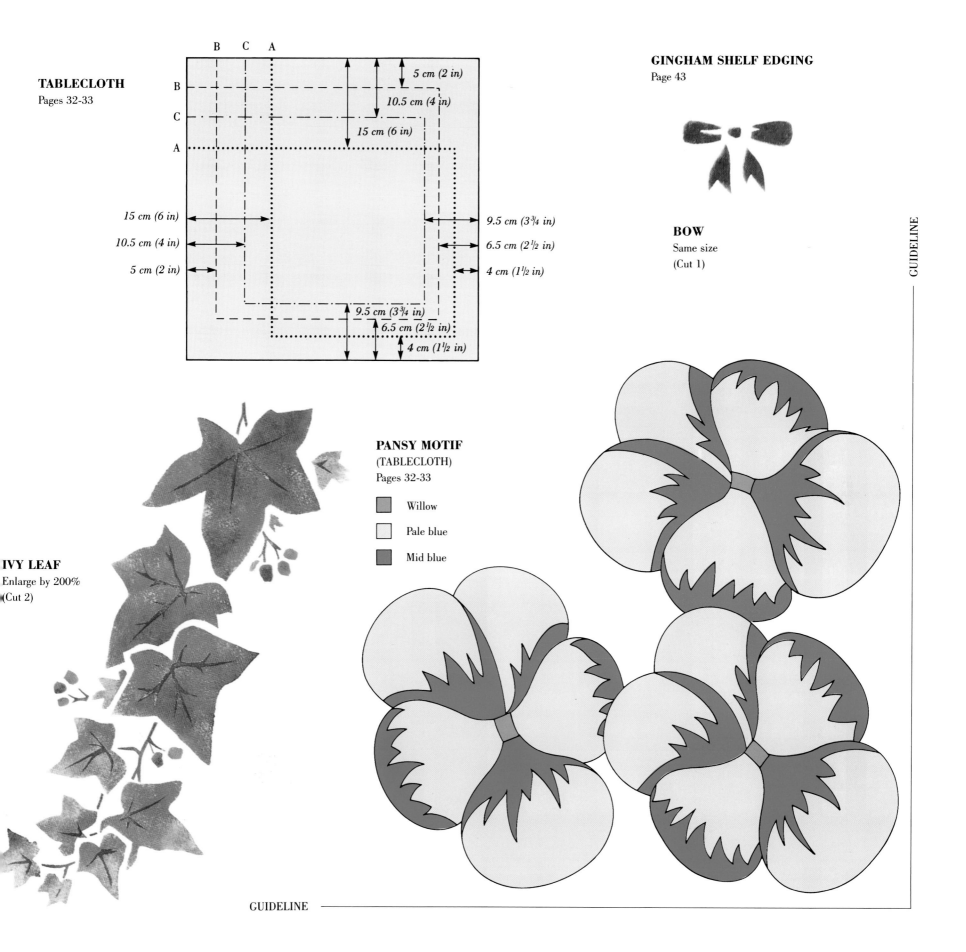

TABLECLOTH
Pages 32-33

B   C   A

B

C

A

5 cm (2 in)

10.5 cm (4 in)

15 cm (6 in)

15 cm (6 in)

10.5 cm (4 in)

5 cm (2 in)

9.5 cm (3¾ in)

6.5 cm (2½ in)

4 cm (1½ in)

9.5 cm (3¾ in)

6.5 cm (2½ in)

4 cm (1½ in)

GINGHAM SHELF EDGING
Page 43

BOW
Same size
(Cut 1)

GUIDELINE

PANSY MOTIF
(TABLECLOTH)
Pages 32-33

Willow

Pale blue

Mid blue

IVY LEAF
Enlarge by 200%
(Cut 2)

GUIDELINE

TARTAN THROW
Pages 36-37

■	75 mm (3 in) wide tartan polyester 3.5 m (4 yd)	■ 50 mm (2 in) wide rust velvet 1.5 m (1¾ yd)	■ 20 mm (¾ in) wide green velvet 2 m (2¼ yd)
■	3 mm (1½ in) wide tartan polyester 4.5 m (5 yd)	■ 50 mm (2 in) wide green velvet 2.5 m (2¾ yd)	■ 20 mm (¾ in) wide rust velvet 3.5 m (4 yd)

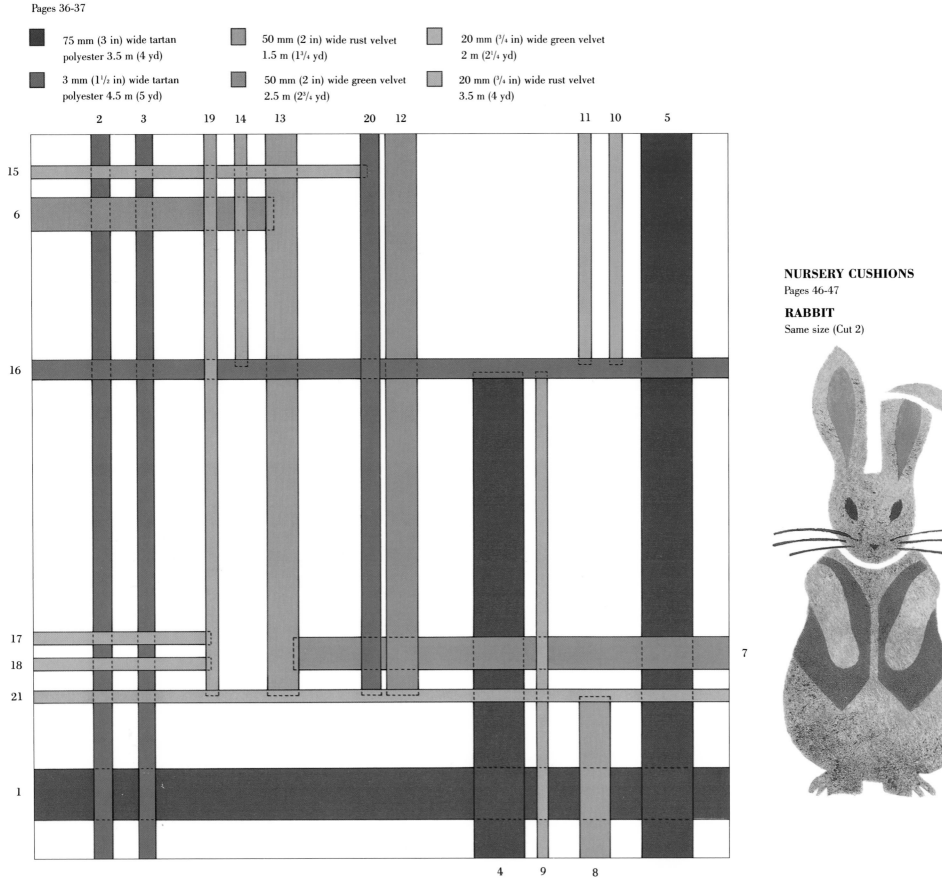

NURSERY CUSHIONS
Pages 46-47

RABBIT
Same size (Cut 2)

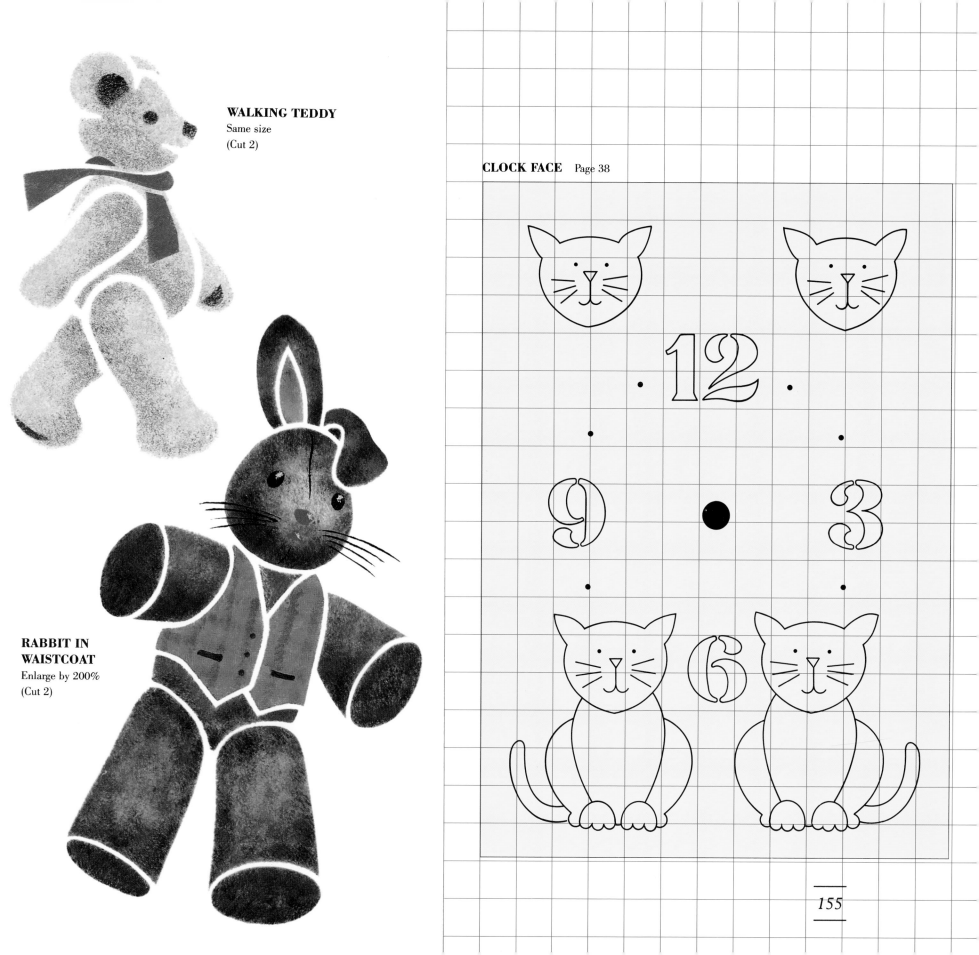

WALKING TEDDY
Same size
(Cut 2)

**RABBIT IN
WAISTCOAT**
Enlarge by 200%
(Cut 2)

CLOCK FACE   Page 38

12

9   3

6

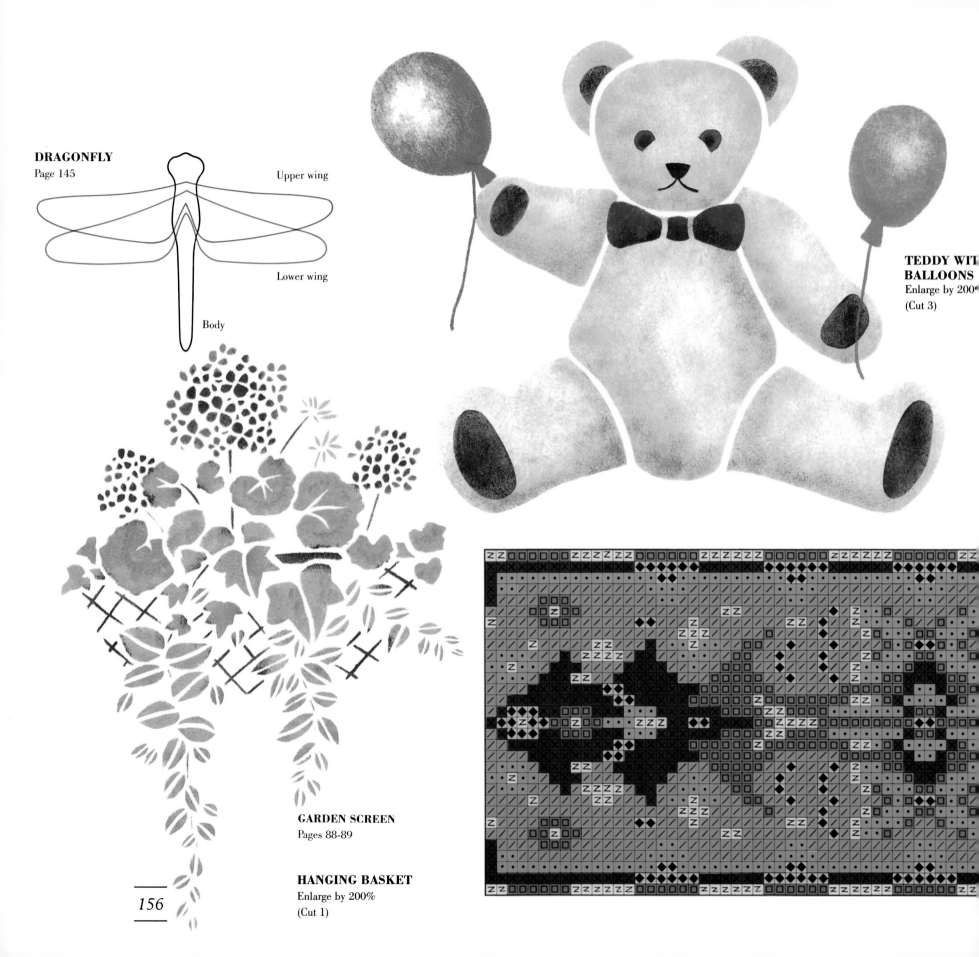

DRAGONFLY
Page 145

Upper wing

Lower wing

Body

TEDDY WIT
BALLOONS
Enlarge by 200%
(Cut 3)

GARDEN SCREEN
Pages 88-89

HANGING BASKET
Enlarge by 200%
(Cut 1)

WALLHANGING

Pages 46-47

38 mm (1¹/₂ in) wide double satin ribbon

◆ Bronze lurex 9 m (10 yd)

36 mm (1²/₅ in) wide double satin ribbon

· Jade 20 m (22 yd)

╱ Airforce blue 40 m (44 yd)

✕ Chocolate 18 m (20 yd)

▢ Terracotta 23 m (25¹/₄ yd)

Z Ochre 14 m (15¹/₂ yd)

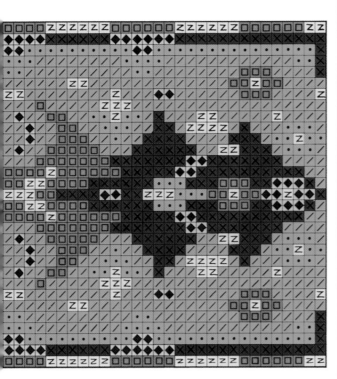

TABLECLOTH DESIGN

Pages 52-53

WALLHANGING

Pages 44-45

**ETHNIC CUSHION –
ELEPHANT**

Pages 56-57

Enlarge by 200%

**NOAH'S ARK
COT QUILT**

Pages 50-51

ELEPHANTS

Enlarge by 150%

(Cut 1)

**ETHNIC CUSHION –
ZEBRA**

Pages 56-57

Enlarge by 200%

LION

Enlarge by 150%

(Cut 3)

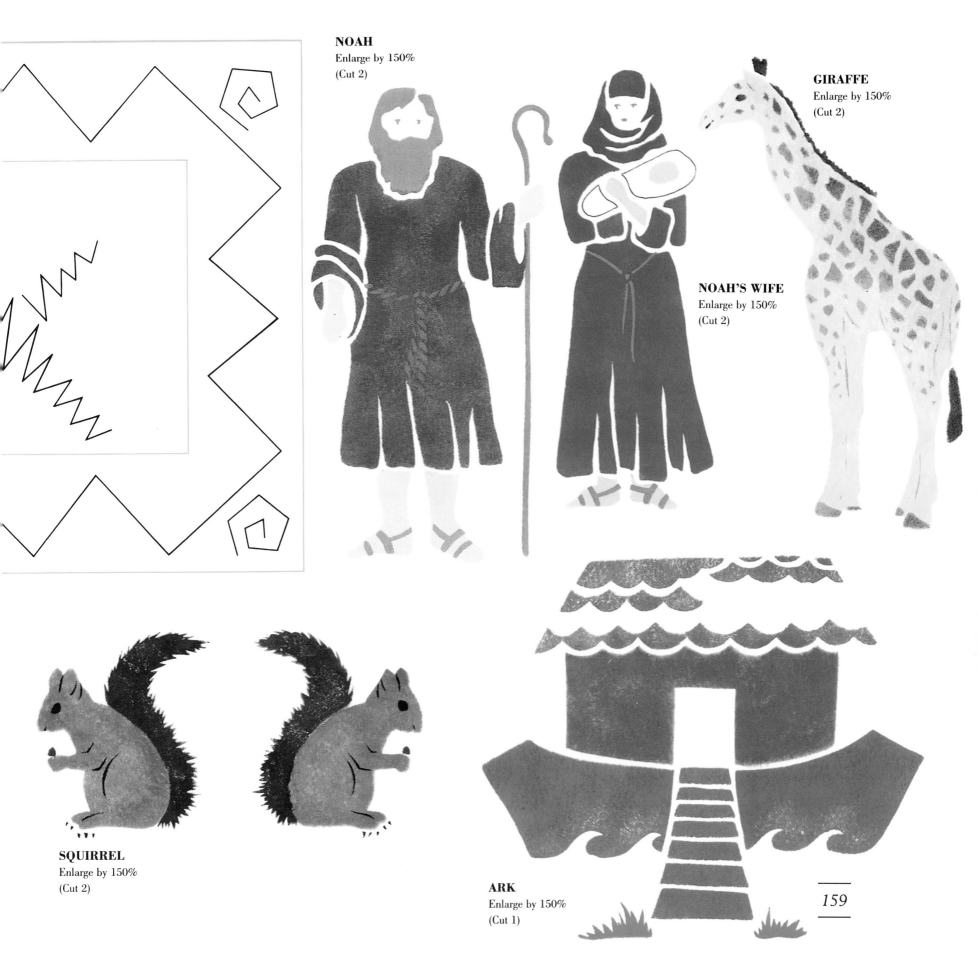

NOAH
Enlarge by 150%
(Cut 2)

NOAH'S WIFE
Enlarge by 150%
(Cut 2)

GIRAFFE
Enlarge by 150%
(Cut 2)

SQUIRREL
Enlarge by 150%
(Cut 2)

ARK
Enlarge by 150%
(Cut 1)

159

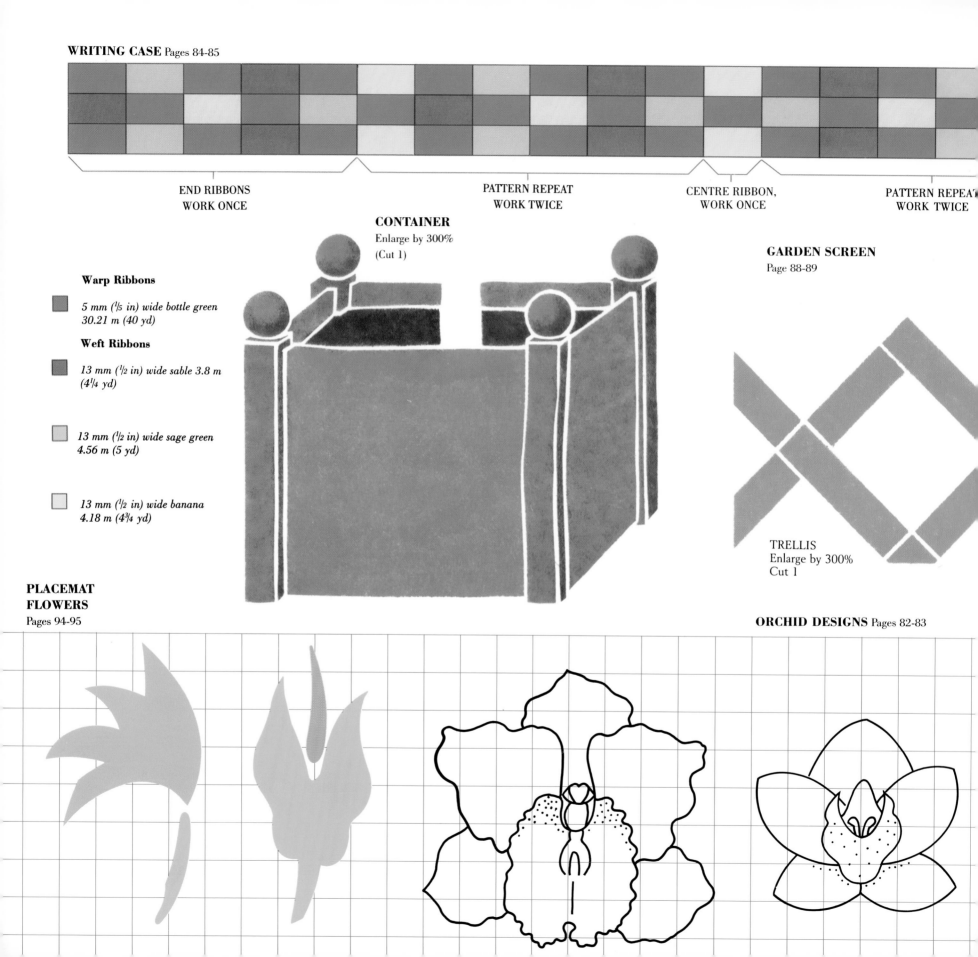

WRITING CASE Pages 84-85

END RIBBONS
WORK ONCE

PATTERN REPEAT
WORK TWICE

CENTRE RIBBON,
WORK ONCE

PATTERN REPEAT
WORK TWICE

CONTAINER
Enlarge by 300%
(Cut 1)

GARDEN SCREEN
Page 88-89

Warp Ribbons

5 mm (¹/₅ in) wide bottle green
30.21 m (40 yd)

Weft Ribbons

13 mm (¹/₂ in) wide sable 3.8 m
(4¹/₄ yd)

13 mm (¹/₂ in) wide sage green
4.56 m (5 yd)

13 mm (¹/₂ in) wide banana
4.18 m (4³/₄ yd)

TRELLIS
Enlarge by 300%
Cut 1

**PLACEMAT
FLOWERS**
Pages 94-95

ORCHID DESIGNS Pages 82-83

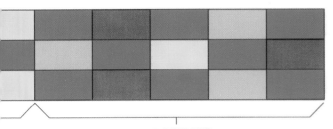

END RIBBON

PATTERN REPEAT

END RIBBONS,
WORK ONCE

HERB POT
Enlarge by 200%
Cut 1

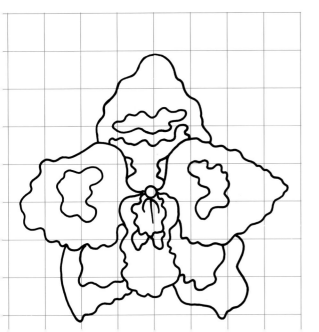

ADVENT CALENDAR
Pages 86-87

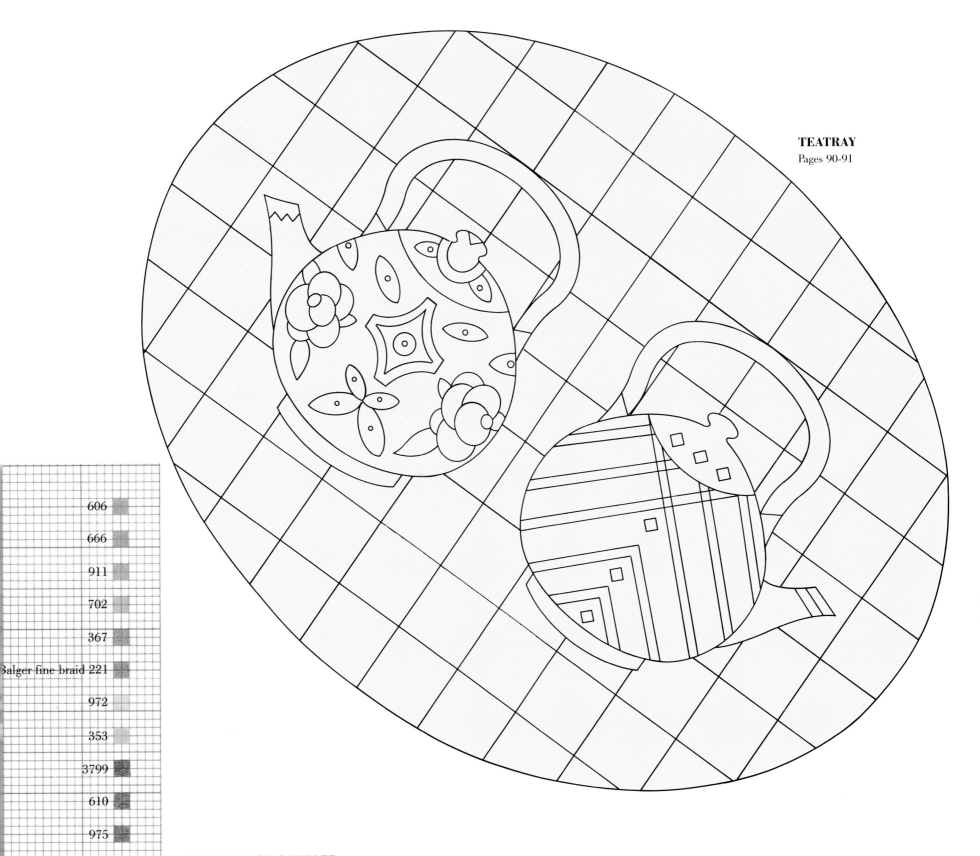

TEATRAY
Pages 90-91

606

666

911

702

367

Balger fine braid 221

972

353

3799

610

975

976

CROSS STITCH SAMPLER
Pages 92-93

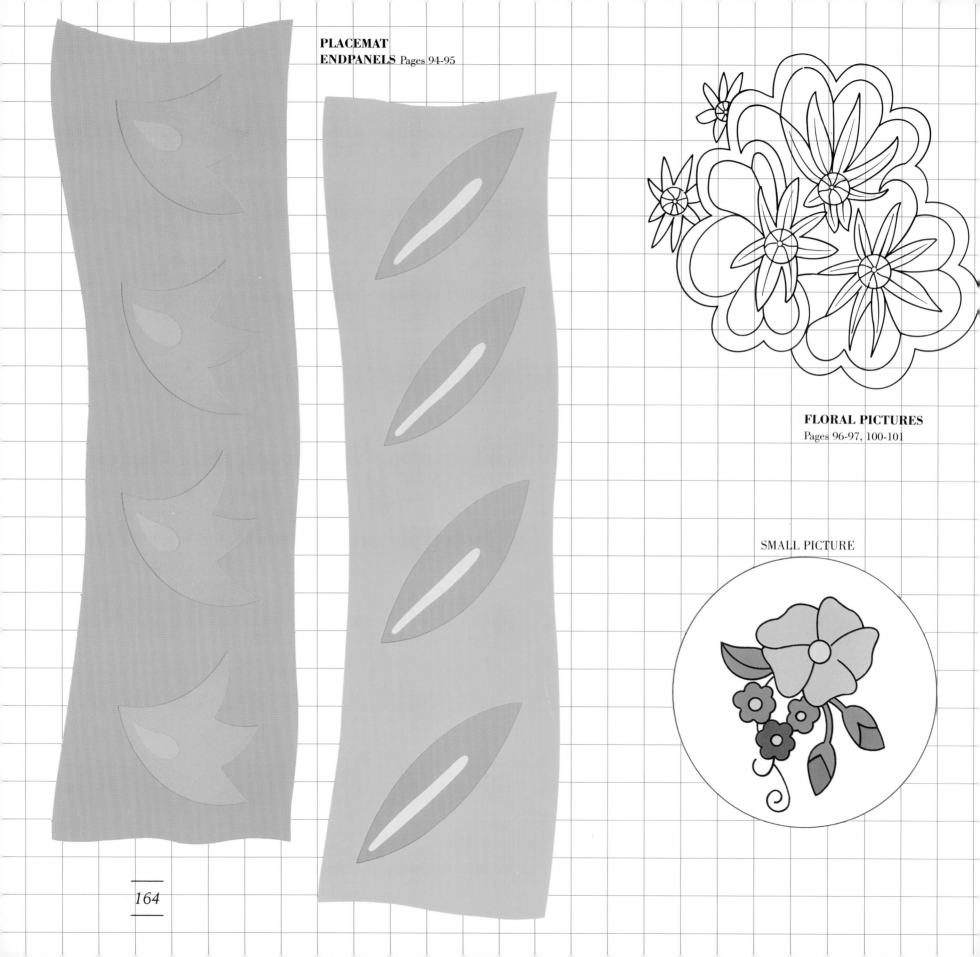

**PLACEMAT
ENDPANELS** Pages 94-95

FLORAL PICTURES
Pages 96-97, 100-101

SMALL PICTURE

164

LARGE PICTURE

MEDIUM PICTURE

SILHOUETTE 1
Same size
Cut 1

SILHOUETTE 2
Same size
Cut 1

FLORAL BOUQUET
Same size
Cut 1

ROSE
Same size
Cut 1

ROSEBUDS
Same size
Cut 1 each

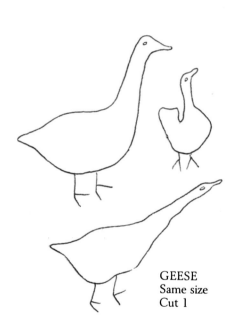

GEESE
Same size
Cut 1

OAK LEAVES
Same size
Cut 1

CHERRIES
Same size
Cut 1

CUTWORK TABLEMAT AND NAPKIN
Pages 98-99

TABLEMAT

NAPKIN ▶

EGYPTIAN BATHROOM
Pages 106-107

FLOWER
Same size
Cut 1

PALM TREE
Same size
Cut 1

FLOWER
Same size
Cut 1

Place on Fold

WATER CARRIER
Same size
Cut 1

SPHINX
Same size
Cut 1

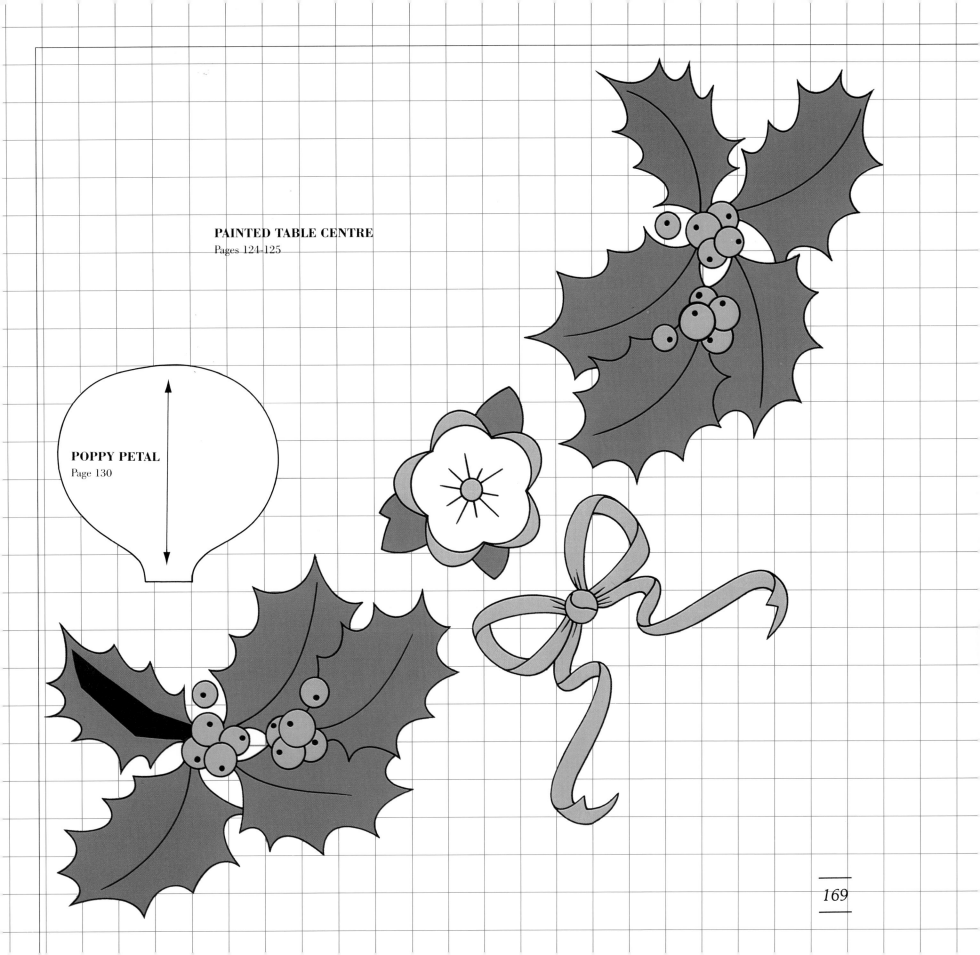

PAINTED TABLE CENTRE
Pages 124-125

POPPY PETAL
Page 130

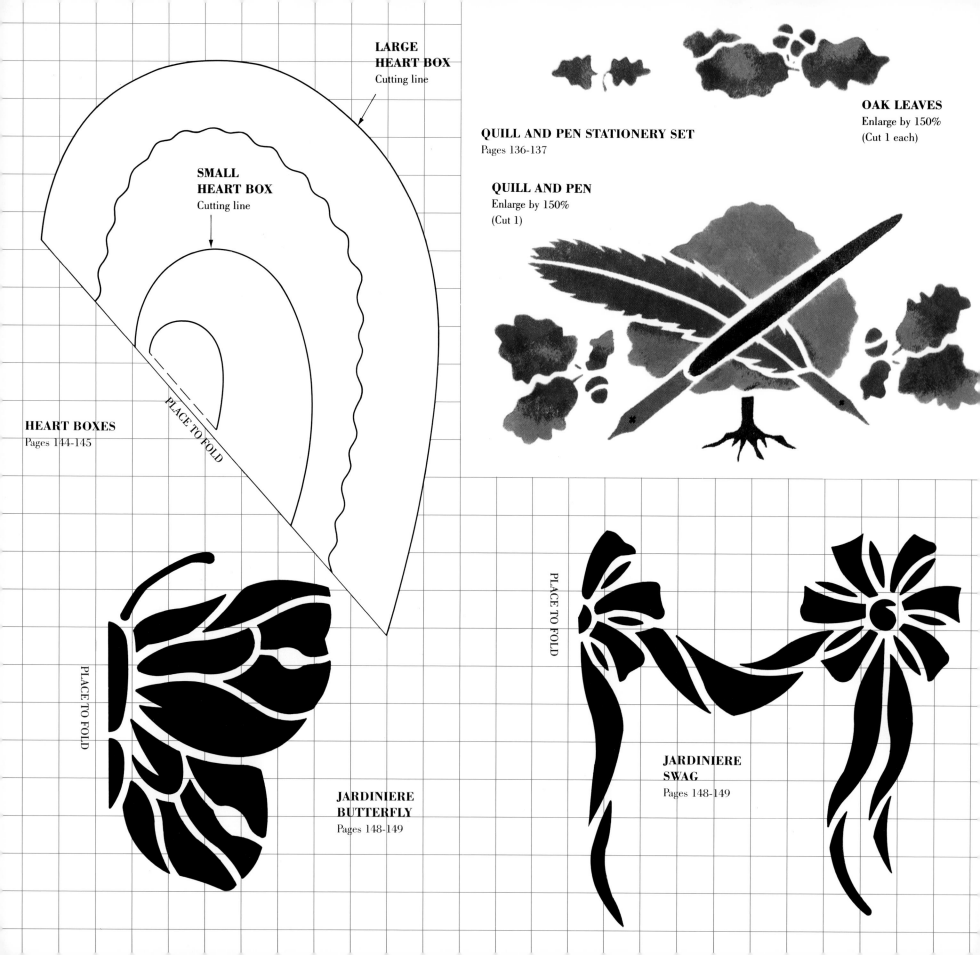

**LARGE
HEART BOX**
Cutting line

**SMALL
HEART BOX**
Cutting line

PLACE TO FOLD

HEART BOXES
Pages 144-145

QUILL AND PEN STATIONERY SET
Pages 136-137

OAK LEAVES
Enlarge by 150%
(Cut 1 each)

QUILL AND PEN
Enlarge by 150%
(Cut 1)

PLACE TO FOLD

**JARDINIERE
BUTTERFLY**
Pages 148-149

PLACE TO FOLD

**JARDINIERE
SWAG**
Pages 148-149

FARMHOUSE KITCHENWARE
Pages 146-147

FLORAL MOTIFS
Same size
(Cut 1 of each)

COW
Same size
(Cut 1)

HEART BOXES
Pages 144-145

SMALL HEART RIM
Page 145

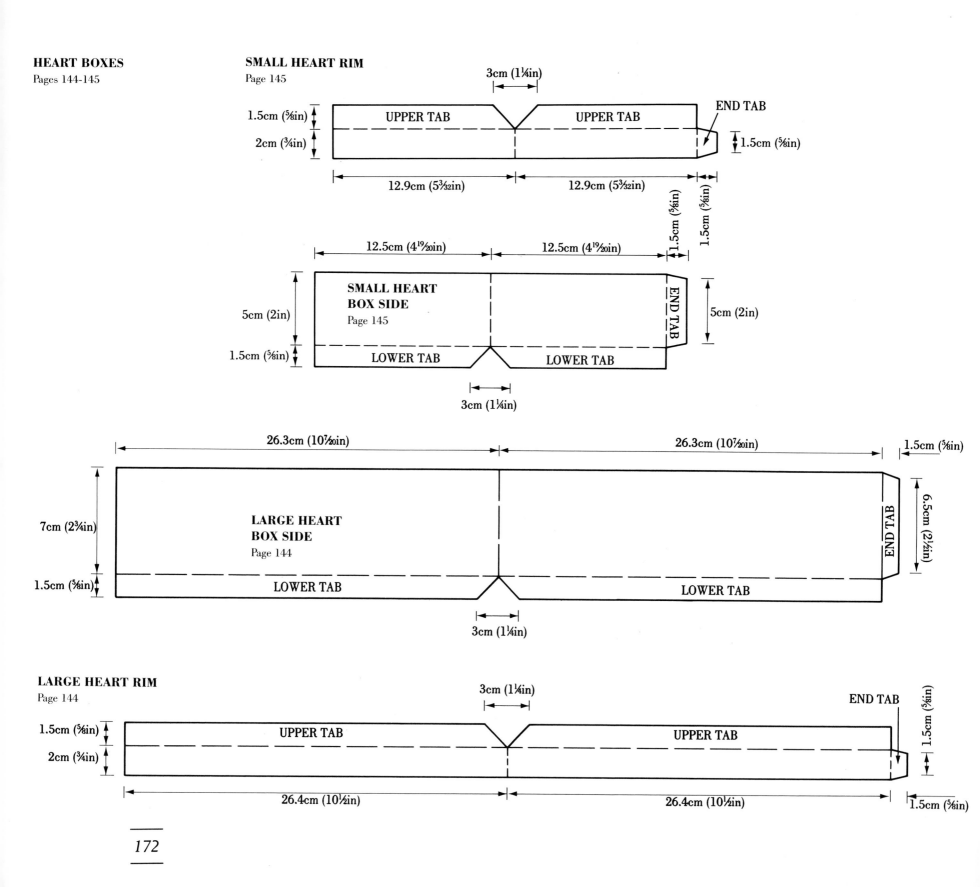

3cm (1¼in)

1.5cm (⅝in)

2cm (¾in)

UPPER TAB

UPPER TAB

END TAB

1.5cm (⅝in)

12.9cm (5³⁄₃₂in)

12.9cm (5³⁄₃₂in)

1.5cm (⅝in)

1.5cm (⅝in)

12.5cm (4¹⁹⁄₂₀in)

12.5cm (4¹⁹⁄₂₀in)

1.5cm (⅝in)

SMALL HEART BOX SIDE
Page 145

5cm (2in)

1.5cm (⅝in)

LOWER TAB

LOWER TAB

END TAB

5cm (2in)

3cm (1¼in)

26.3cm (10⁷⁄₂₀in)

26.3cm (10⁷⁄₂₀in)

1.5cm (⅝in)

LARGE HEART BOX SIDE
Page 144

7cm (2¾in)

1.5cm (⅝in)

LOWER TAB

LOWER TAB

END TAB

6.5cm (2½in)

3cm (1¼in)

LARGE HEART RIM
Page 144

3cm (1¼in)

END TAB

1.5cm (⅝in)

2cm (¾in)

UPPER TAB

UPPER TAB

1.5cm (⅝in)

26.4cm (10½in)

26.4cm (10½in)

1.5cm (⅝in)

Suppliers

Thanks to:

DMC Creative World
Pullman Road,
Wigstone,
Leics. LE18 2DY.

The Handicraft Shop,
Northgate, Canterbury.
CT1 1BE.

Framecraft Miniatures Ltd,
372-376 Summer Lane,
Hockley, Birmingham.
B19 3QA.

Credits

Publishing Manager: Will Steeds
Editor: Sue Wilkinson
Additional Editorial Work: Jo Richardson
Design: Phil Gorton
Photographers: Steve Tanner, Nelson Hargreaves
Production: Ruth Arthur, Karen Staff, Neil Randles, Paul Randles
Production Director: Gerald Hughes

Contributors:
Annette Claxton pages 32-33, 40-41
Jan Eaton pages 34-35, 38-39, 44-45, 52-53, 86-87, 90-91, 94-97, 102-105, 108-109, 130-131
Anita Harrison pages 30-31, 36-37, 48-49, 54-57, 88-89, 92-93, 100-101, 156-157
Jane McDonnell pages 116-117, 120-121
Jane Newdick pages 62-63, 66-71, 74-75, 80-83
Cheryl Owen pages 98-99, 134-141, 144-151, 154-155
Gillie Spargo pages 28-29, 42-43, 46-47, 50-51, 106-107, 110-111, 142-143, 152-153
Pamela Westland pages 60-61, 64-65, 72-73, 76-79, 114-115, 118-119, 122-123